Folens
Science in Action
Year 1

Author:
Helen Whittaker

Boscombe Road, Dunstable, LU5 4RL.
Email: folens@folens.com

Ireland: Folens Publishers, Greenhills Road, Tallaght, Dublin 24.
Email: info@folens.ie

Poland: JUKA, ul. Renesansowa 38, Warsaw 01-905.

Editors: Gaynor Spry and Nancy Candlin
Layout artist: Patricia Hollingsworth
Illustrations: Lee Sullivan
Cover design: Martin Cross

First published 2004 by Folens Limited.

Every effort has been made to contact copyright holders of material used in this publication. If any copyright holder has been overlooked, we should be pleased to make any necessary arrangements.

British Library Cataloguing in Publication Data. A catalogue record for this publication is available from the British Library.

ISBN 1 84303 574 X

Contents

Introduction 3
Assessment Grid: Scientific Enquiry 5

Unit A – OURSELVES 6–19
Assessment Grid 6

Lesson 1
Our Senses 7
Resource Sheet 'Word Cards for Unit 1A' 8
A1 Our Senses 9

Lesson 2
Growing and Changing 10
A2 Growing and Changing 11

Lesson 3
Measuring Heights 12
A3 Measuring Heights 13

Lesson 4
The Same But Different 14
A4 Eye Colour 15

Lesson 5
Animals in Motion 16
Resource Sheet 'How Animals Move' 17

Lesson 6
Eating and Drinking 18
A6 Animal Food Riddles 19

Unit B – GROWING PLANTS 20–33
Assessment Grid 20

Lesson 1
Plants Everywhere 21
Resource Sheet 'Word Cards for Unit 1B' 22
B1 Plants Everywhere 23

Lesson 2
Plant Parts 24
Resource Sheet 'Plant Parts' 25

Lesson 3
Growing Plants 26
B3 Growing Plants 27

Lesson 4
Roots 28
B4 Roots 29

Lesson 5
The Light Stuff 30
B5 Do Plants Need Light to Grow? 31

Lesson 6
What Do We Know About Plants? 32
B6 Our Big Book of Plants 33

Unit C – SORTING AND USING MATERIALS 34–47
Assessment Grid 34

Lesson 1
Exploring Materials 35
Resource Sheet 'Word Cards for Unit 1C' 36
C1 Exploring Materials 37

Lesson 2
Identifying Materials 38
C2 Materials Hunt 39

Lesson 3
Sorting Materials 40
C3 Sorting Materials 41

Lesson 4
Choosing Materials 42
C4 Wrapping a Parcel 43

Lesson 5
Magnetic Materials 44
C5 Magnetic or Not? 45

Lesson 6
Is It Waterproof? 46
C6 Is It Waterproof? 47

Unit D – LIGHT AND DARK 48–57
Assessment Grid 48

Lesson 1
Light Sources 49
Resource Sheet 'Word Cards for Unit 1D' 50
Resource Sheet 'Is It a Light Source?' 51

Lesson 2
The Sun 52
D2 The Sun 53

Lesson 3
Can You See in the Dark? 54

Lesson 4
Being Seen at Night 55

Lesson 5
What Do We Know About Light and Dark? 56
D5 Light Quiz 57

Unit E – PUSHES AND PULLS 58–67
Assessment Grid 58

Lesson 1
How Do Things Move? 59
Resource Sheet 'Word Cards for Unit 1E' 60
E1 How Do We Move? 61

Lesson 2
Starting and Stopping 62

Lesson 3
What Makes It Move? 63
Resource Sheet 'What Makes It Move?' 64
E3 What Makes It Move? 65

Lesson 4
Windmills 66
Resource Sheet 'Windmills' 67

Unit F – SOUND AND HEARING 68–79
Assessment Grid 68

Lesson 1
Identifying Sounds 69
Resource Sheet 'Word Cards for Unit 1F' 70

Lesson 2
Making and Describing sounds 71
F2 Making and Describing Sounds 72
Resource Sheet 'Sounds Word Bank' 73

Lesson 3
Hearing Sounds 74
Resource Sheet 'Hearing Sounds' 75

Lesson 4
Sounds Near and Far 76
Resource Sheet 'Sounds' 77

Lesson 5
Investigating Sounds 78
F5 Which Sound Travels Further? 79

Record Form 80

Introduction

Folens Science in Action is a complete course in primary science. It meets the requirements for the National Curriculum in England and Wales, and is compatible with the scheme of work published in England by the Qualifications and Curriculum Authority (QCA).

Aims of Folens Science in Action

The overall aim of the book is that children should come to understand, appreciate and respect the scientific approach to understanding the world, recognise how science affects their lives and investigate scientific questions with enthusiasm.

Children should:

- be taught knowledge, skills and understanding in science through a range of domestic and environmental contexts that are familiar and of interest to them
- look at the part science has played in the development of many useful things
- use a range of sources of information and data, including ICT-based sources
- use first-hand and secondary data to carry out a range of investigative tasks, including complete investigations
- use simple scientific language to communicate ideas and to name and describe living things, materials, phenomena and processes recognise that there are hazards in living things, materials and physical processes, and assess risks and take action to reduce risks to themselves and others

The Structure of Folens Science in Action and the Materials

Year 1 is divided into six units of work. The units are based on those in the scheme of work published by the QCA in England. Each unit is intended to occupy 6–9 hours of teaching time and is focused on a specific aspect of science. You can use the units in any order you prefer.
We recommend:

Autumn Term	Spring Term	Summer Term
Units A and D	Units C and E	Units F and B

One unit comprises up to six lessons. Most are intended to be taught in a single session. In specific cases, however, because investigations need to take place over an extended period, the lesson may need to be spread over more than one session.

The unit begins with an indication of the main scientific ideas covered in the unit. These ideas are covered at varying levels through the programme as a whole. The time you will need to allocate to the unit is also shown.

Each unit also contains a page of word cards covering appropriate vocabulary. They can be enlarged on a photocopier, either at 141% (A4 to A3) or on to two sheets of A3 at 200% (A5 to A3). To extend the life of the word cards, copy them directly on to card or laminate them.

For each lesson, a full lesson plan is provided, and the Science Background and Learning Objectives are made clear. The lessons begin with an Introduction, normally intended to be carried out with the whole class, which provides the context for the work of the lesson. This is followed by a Main Activity, usually requiring work in small groups. The whole-class Plenary is used to draw the work of the lesson together. This discussion is important for clarifying what has been learned, and you should ensure that enough time is allocated for this. During this time you can make judgements about whether the lesson objectives have been achieved and take the opportunity for corrective action, if necessary. Throughout, there are examples of questions to ask the children and of what the children will need to be told. You should adapt these to suit the children in your class.

The children's work is supported by photocopiable pupil sheets, which are fully referenced in the lesson plans.

Introduction

Progression and Differentiation

Folens Science in Action has been carefully constructed to ensure that scientific ideas are introduced and developed systematically over the course of the programme. Key objectives are identified in each lesson by a ■. It is expected that the large majority of children will achieve these objectives. Where appropriate, there are suggestions on how to differentiate the work to ensure it meets the needs of all pupils. These are found under the headings **Differentiation** and **Extension** in the *Main Activity* section. Resource sheets, marked by **RS**, are used to support the children's work both during the lesson and as they work on the pupil sheets.

Further differentiation is possible in the scientific enquiries that the children undertake. Different children can address the same investigative task with different amounts of direction and support, and they can take the investigation to different levels. The lessons are planned so that most children will make appropriate progress in enquiry skills. However, you should use your ongoing assessment to identify those children who need help as well as those who may be prompted to move on to a higher level of skill.

Assessment and Record-keeping

Progress in scientific enquiry can be assessed as opportunities arise in the course of investigative work using the *Assessment Grid: Scientific Enquiry* on the next page. The levels are equivalent to the National Curriculum levels used in England, Wales and Northern Ireland to measure the children's progress.

The *What to Look For* section in each lesson gives a more specific indication of the evidence you should look for in judging whether the children have achieved the lesson objectives. At the end of the work on a particular unit, you should use both the *Assessment Grid: Scientific Enquiry* and the relevant unit Assessment Grid (found on each unit's introductory page) to assess the level of the children's scientific knowledge and understanding. Use the grids to come to an overall judgement of the level reached by individual children, based on the set of descriptions that most closely match the child's performance overall.

By the end of Year 1 most children will be expected to achieve Level 2. More able children may achieve Level 3. Less able children may still be working at Level 1. Some children may not yet have achieved Level 1 in all areas and in this case their achievement in these areas should be recorded as a W (working towards Level 1).

The Record Form on page 80 can be used to keep a cumulative record of the children's attainment throughout the course of the academic year.

Assessment Grid: Scientific Enquiry

Children working at level 1 typically:	Children working at level 2 typically:	Children working at level 3 typically:
Planning		
• Respond appropriately to simple features of objects, living things and events.	• Respond to suggestions about how to find things out. • With help, make their own suggestions about how to collect data to answer questions. • With help, say what they think will happen.	• Respond to suggestions about how to find things out. • Put forward their own ideas about how to find the answer to a question. • Recognise why it is important to collect data to answer questions.
Obtaining and Presenting Evidence		
• Observe and describe objects, living things and events.	• Use simple texts, with help, to find information. • Use simple equipment provided. • Make observations related to their task. • Observe and compare objects, living things and events.	• Use simple texts to find information. • Make relevant observations. • Measure quantities, such as length or mass, using a range of simple equipment. • Where appropriate, they carry out a fair test with some help, recognising and explaining why it is fair. • Record their observations in a variety of ways.
Considering Evidence and Evaluating		
• Communicate their findings in simple ways (for example, talking about their work, through drawings or simple charts).	• Describe their observations using scientific vocabulary. • Record observations, using simple tables when appropriate. • Say whether what happened was what they expected.	• Provide explanations for observations and for simple patterns in recorded measurements. • Communicate their findings in a scientific way. • Suggest improvements in their work.

Unit A

Ourselves

Scientific Enquiry: • Ask questions and decide how they might find answers to them. • Explore, using the senses of sight, hearing, smell, touch and taste as appropriate, and make and record observations and measurements. • Compare what happened with what they expected would happen, and try to explain it, drawing on their knowledge and understanding.
Life Processes and Living Things: • Recognise the differences between things that are living and things that have never been alive. • Know that animals, including humans, move, feed, grow, use their senses and reproduce. • Recognise and compare the main external parts of the bodies of humans and other animals. • Know about the senses that enable humans and other animals to be aware of the world around them. • Recognise similarities and differences between themselves and others, and treat others with sensitivity.
Approximate Teaching Time: 9 hours

Assessment Grid

Unit 1A

	At level 1, children typically:	**At level 2, children typically:**	**At level 3, children typically:**
Life Process and Living Things	• recognise and name external parts of the body. • communicate observations of a range of animals in terms of features. • recognise and identify a range of common animals.	• use their knowledge about living things to describe the basic conditions that animals need in order to survive. • recognise that living things grow and reproduce. • sort living things into groups, using simple features. • describe the basis for their groupings.	• use their knowledge and understanding of basic life processes when they describe differences between living and non-living things. • provide simple explanations for changes in living things.

Our Senses

Science Background

Using their senses to find out about their environment is an essential survival mechanism shared by all animals.

Learning Objectives

Children should:

- know that humans have bodies with similar parts.
- know that we have five senses that allow us to find out about the world around us.

Resources

- Blindfold
- 'Smell' table: six covered 'smell pots' with non-toxic contents, numbered 1 to 6
- 'Taste' table: six packets of crisps in different flavours on six paper plates, numbered 1 to 6
- 'Touch' table: six everyday objects in six feely bags or boxes, numbered 1 to 6
- 'Sound' table: sound effects CD, CD player and headphones
- 'Sight' table: six interesting objects, six magnifying glasses, and paper and pencils for observational drawing
- Labels for each table
- Tray of 'feely objects' (soft, hard, rough, smooth, warm to touch, cold to touch, etc.)
- Pupil sheet A1 (copied to A3 and cut up)

Introduction

Play a game of 'Simon Says', pointing to different parts of the body. Make sure that eyes, nose, ears, tongue and skin are all included in the game. Focusing on the five sense organs, ask: *How does this part of your body help you to find out about the world around you?* Using the cards from the Pupil sheet 'Our Senses', ask children to come out and match the cards to the correct part of the body. Build the cards into an information table about the senses.

Main Activity

Set up the five activity tables, labelling each one with the name of the relevant sense. Organise the class into five groups. *Can you guess what each object or sound is?* Explain that on the 'sight' table they will not need to identify the objects. Instead, they will first look closely at an object using a magnifying glass and then draw it in detail. Give each group about five minutes on each table.

Differentiation: More able children could write down what they think each object is on the smell, taste and touch tables. Others could explain their ideas verbally.

After every group has completed all the activities, discuss the children's ideas. Ask, for example: *Did you identify this sound on the tape? Which part of your body did you use to work it out? Which sense were you using when you were using the feely bag or box? Which things were easy to work out? Which things were hard to work out? Why?* Refer to the senses information table made from the Pupil sheet in the Introduction.

How do your senses help to keep you safe? Reinforce the idea that our senses are often used in combination. For example: *Which senses do you use when you cross the road? Which senses tell you whether food is safe to eat?*

Plenary

Children can forget that the organ of touch is the whole of the skin and not just the fingers. To reinforce this idea, blindfold a volunteer. Ask another child to choose an object from the tray and use it to touch the blindfolded child on a piece of exposed skin. Ask the blindfolded child: *Where did that touch you? Was it soft or hard? Was it rough or smooth? Was it cold or warm?* When the blindfold is off, ask them to pick out the object that touched them.

Ask the children what happens if one of the senses is not working properly. This could lead into a sensitive discussion about visual and hearing problems encountered by elderly relatives, or about children who are deaf or blind.

What to Look For

Children can identify and locate different parts of their body, including sense organs. They can say what each sense organ does. Some children can name the five senses

⚠ Ensure that all the objects you use have no sharp edges, are unlikely to break and are non-toxic. To discourage children from ingesting the substances on the 'smell' table, cover each pot securely and make the holes in the lid very small.

RS

Word Cards for Unit 1A

eyes	nose
ears	tongue
skin	sight
smell	hearing
taste	touch
order	sort
oldest	tallest
shortest	youngest

Our Senses

Body part	What it does	Sense
	I hear with my ears.	hearing
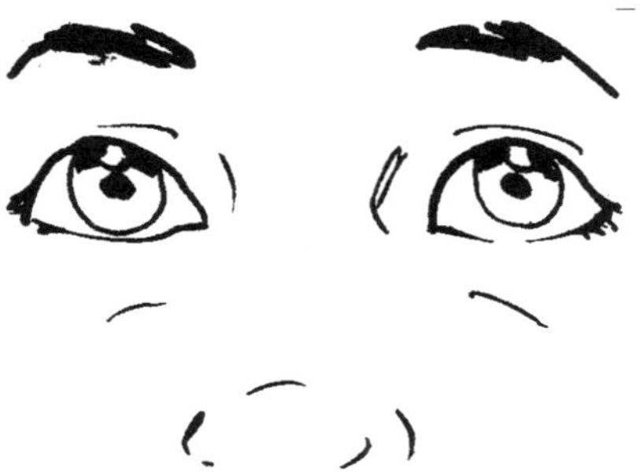	I see with my eyes.	sight
	I smell with my nose.	smell
	I taste with my tongue.	taste
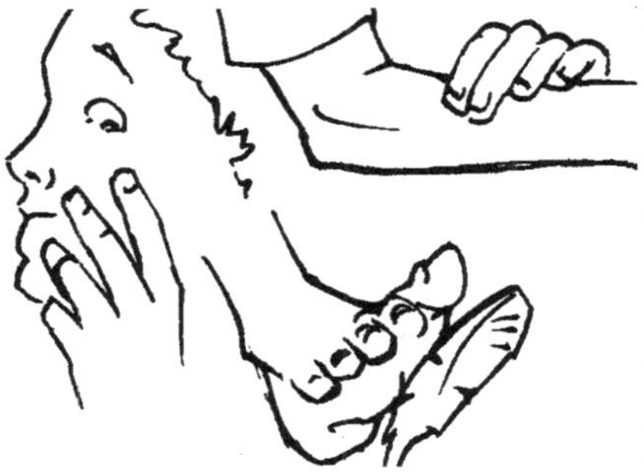	I feel with my skin.	touch

Growing and Changing

Science Background

Growth is a common characteristic of all living things. Children need to know that all animals grow, and that as well as an increase in size, growth may involve other changes. A common misconception at this age is that humans aren't animals, and some children do not yet recognise that invertebrates (for example, snails, starfish, jellyfish, insects, spiders and earthworms) are animals. Others may not realise that some classes of vertebrates (for example, fish or birds) are properly described as animals.

Learning Objectives

Children should:

- know that the term 'animal' includes humans.
- know that all animals, including humans, grow and change as they become older.
- make and communicate observations and comparisons of humans and other animals.
- match young and adult of the same animal.

Resources

- Small whiteboards, pens and wipes
- A collection of photographs of people the children are familiar with, showing growth and change (for example, a recent class photograph of the oldest children in the school and, for comparison, their very first class photograph; or old photos of themselves that the children bring from home)
- Pupil sheet A2 (including one large copy or transparency)
- Scissors
- Glue sticks
- Plain paper or science books

Introduction

Give out the whiteboards, pens and wipes and ask the children to draw an animal quickly. Do this in three or four rounds, asking for a different broad category of animal in each round. For example, first ask the children to draw an animal that flies, then one that can swim, then one with two legs, and finally one that you might find in the garden. Explain that one thing all animals have in common is that they grow and change as they get older.

Main Activity

Look at the collection of photographs (see Resources above). *How have people changed from one photograph to another? How have they changed since they were born? How might they continue to change as they grow older?*

Give children copies of the Pupil sheet A2. Ask them to match the young to the adult animal by cutting and sticking the pictures and animal name labels onto another sheet of paper or into their science books.

Differentiation: For more able children, omit the list of words at the bottom of the sheet and ask them to label the pictures themselves. Some children may need help reading the list of words. Less able children could work in pairs to complete the task.
Extension: Ask the children to write the way each one has changed (for example, 'got bigger', 'changed shape', 'changed markings') next to the pictures of the adult animals.

Plenary

Display a large copy or transparency of Pupil sheet A2. Play a game of 'Guess the Animal'. Describe the characteristics of one of the adult animals and ask the children to name it. Label each named animal. Compare the different adult animals by asking, for example: *How is the tiger different to the frog? How is it the same?*

Ask the children to explain how, in the Main Activity, they paired the animals and why. Finally, ask the children to tell you the ways in which each animal has changed from young to adult.

What to Look For
Children can name animals from descriptions. They know that humans are a type of animal. They can compare animals with each other. Some children use comparisons based on knowledge of animal behaviour as well as visible differences. They match the young and adult of each animal correctly and describe changes that take place as the animal gets older.

Growing and Changing

cub	tadpole	sheep
chicken	baby	caterpillar
butterfly	tiger	woman
lamb	frog	chick

Measuring Heights

Science Background

In the previous lesson, children learned that all animals grow as they mature. Because of this, some children may believe that older children are necessarily taller. They may not realise that children grow at different rates and that this leads to differences in height. This lesson needs handling with sensitivity. Some children can be self-conscious about their height, particularly if they are especially tall or short for their age.

Learning Objectives

Children should:

- ask questions and make suggestions about growing and getting older.
- make observations and comparisons of height.
- decide whether their prediction was correct.

Resources

- A soft toy (for example, a giraffe called Geraldine)
- Class list in birthday order
- Objects of about 10cm in length to use as non-standard units of measurement (for example, place value 'ten sticks')
- Four cards, reading 'oldest', 'youngest', 'tallest' and 'shortest'
- Pupil sheet A3, including one large copy or transparency

Introduction

Introduce the soft toy character. Tell the children her name and explain that she is going to help with the lesson today. Tell them that Geraldine is interested in finding out all their heights, but that first she wants to know whether the children can arrange people in height order.

Ask four or five children to come up to the front. Ask the rest of the class to put these children in order, from tallest to shortest. Do the same for another group of children and ask the others to order them the other way around (from shortest to tallest.) Ask questions which require the children to make comparisons, for example: *Who is shorter than Sonia? Who is taller than Abdul? Is Sam taller or shorter than Ellie?*

Main Activity

Explain that Geraldine has an idea that she would like them to test out. She knows that children grow as they get older and she thinks that the older children in the class will be taller. *Do you agree with Geraldine? Why? Why not?*

Ask the children how they could test out Geraldine's idea. Hopefully someone will suggest they all line up in age order. Give the oldest and youngest children cards that read 'oldest' and 'youngest'. Call out the children's names in age order and ask them to line up in a circle so that everyone can see the whole class. *Who should be given the cards that read 'tallest' and 'shortest'? Who is the oldest? Who is the tallest? Are they the same? Who is the youngest? Who is the shortest? Are they the same? Is the line in age order? Is the line in height order? What did Geraldine think would happen? Was Geraldine right? Is this what you expected?*

Say: *I wonder how tall Geraldine is?* Ask the children first to estimate and then watch as you use the non-standard unit to measure her. Record her height to the nearest whole unit on the large copy of the Pupil sheet A3. Then measure a child in the same way. Organise groups of no more than six to record height measurements of everyone in their group.

Differentiation: Ask more able children to measure each other in centimetres, and to record these results in a table. Less able children may need help with making and recording measurements.
Extension: Ask children to write the names of the people on their table in height order.

Plenary

Look at the height graphs produced by each group and ask questions about the data, such as: *Who is the tallest in this group? How much shorter is Ben than Lauren? How many children are taller than 11 units?* Compare results from two or more groups.

What to Look For

Children can compare their measured height with that of other children, and say whether they are taller or shorter. They recognise that the oldest children in the class are not necessarily the tallest and say whether this was what they expected.

A3

Measuring Heights

Name: ______________________________ Date: ____________________

Height in ______________

14						
13						
12						
11						
10						
9						
8						
7						
6						
5						
4						
3						
2						
1						

Names

The Same But Different

Science Background

Most physical differences between people are programmed by their genes, and yet from a genetic viewpoint human beings are remarkably similar. Compare the genetic code of any two humans and it is likely to be about 99.9% identical. It is the differences in a mere 0.1% of our genes which create the remarkable diversity of human life.

Learning Objectives

Children should:

- know that there are differences between humans.
- collect and organise data and present it in a chart.

Resources

- An infant graphing computer program (for example, RM Starting Graph) or flipchart and coloured pens
- Flipchart or whiteboard
- Pupil sheet A4

Introduction

Play a game to start the children thinking about the similarities and differences between them. Read out a statement and ask the children to indicate whether they think it is true (thumbs up) or false (thumbs down). Example statements: *You all use your eyes to see.* (True) *You all have blue eyes.* (False) *You all have two feet.* (True) *You all have the same size feet.* (False) *You all have hair on your heads.* (True) *You all have blond hair.* (False) *You are all growing taller.* (True) *You are all the same height.* (False)

Discuss both similarities and differences, recording the differences on the board, for example: 'eye colour', 'foot size', 'hair colour', 'height'. Ask children to suggest other ways in which they differ and add these to the list.

Main Activity

Choose a difference from those listed, for example, hair colour, and collect data. Use an infant graphing program or create a table and pictogram (or bar chart) on a flipchart. First, fill in a table with the data then ask the children to help you complete the pictogram or bar chart using this data. Ask questions about the chart: *How many people have black hair? How do you know? Which part of the chart shows you that? Which is the most common hair colour? Which is the least common? How many more people have brown hair than blonde hair? What else does the chart tell you?*

How could we find out about eye colours in our class? Prompt the class to decide on a method of data collection, then conduct the survey and, together, enter the data in an appropriate table on a flipchart or whiteboard. Back in their seats, making sure that everyone can see the data table, ask the children to fill in the pictogram (or bar chart) on the Pupil sheet A4 using the class data.

Differentiation: Less able children may find drawing an eye in every box difficult and time consuming so this group could produce a bar chart or tick chart. More able children can collect data about shoe size, and then create their own pictogram or bar chart.

Plenary

Ask questions about the eye colour data, encouraging children to use their own completed pictograms (or bar charts) to find out the answers: *How many people have brown eyes? Which is the most common eye colour? Which is the least common? How many more people have blue eyes than hazel eyes? What else does the chart tell you?*

What to Look For

Children can collect data and record it in a simple table. They can transfer this data to a pictogram or bar chart. They can answer questions about the data they have collected.

Eye Colour

Name: ______________________ Date: ______________

Eye colour	Number of children
brown	
blue	
green	
hazel	
other	

Number of children

14					
13					
12					
11					
10					
9					
8					
7					
6					
5					
4					
3					
2					
1					

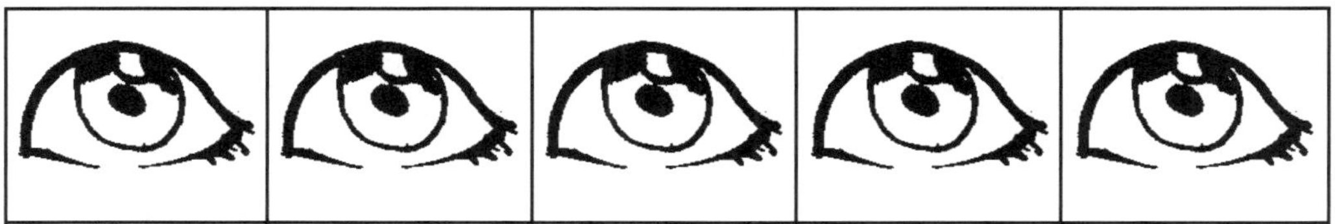

brown	blue	green	hazel	other

Key

 = 1 child

Eye colour

Animals in Motion

Science Background

Movement is a common characteristic shared by all animals. Basic survival instincts, such as finding food, escaping predators and finding a mate, dictate much of an animal's movement. Methods of movement vary widely between different species, and most animals have a range of different types of movement which they use in different situations. For example, a zebra will move very differently when it is grazing compared to when it is being hunted by a lion!

Learning Objectives

Children should:

- know that all animals move, including humans.
- make observations of and comparisons between the ways animals move.
- use observations of animals to sort them into groups, explaining criteria chosen.

Resources

- Whiteboard
- Video, DVD or internet clips which show animals, including humans, in motion. The BBC Nature website has webcam archives for a variety of animals at www.bbc.co.uk/nature/animals/webcams.
- Books illustrating the way animals move, for example, *Animals on the Move* by Gallimard Jeunesse, Sonia Black and Pierre De Hugo (Scholastic); *How Do Animals Move?* By Bobbie Kalman (Crabtree); *Runners, Sliders, Bouncers, Climbers!* by Nick Bantock (Disney Press)
- Resource Sheet 'How Animals Move', including a large copy or transparency
- A3 paper, scissors and glue sticks

Introduction

Tell the children that today they will be learning about the ways in which animals move and that they will be looking at a real, live animal. Ask for one volunteer to come up to the front, and ask the class: *What sort of animal is this?* (Human) *How does this animal move? Which parts of its body does it use to help it move? Does it move in different ways? When does it move in different ways? How many different words can you think of to describe the ways it moves?* Collect the children's suggestions on the board, for example: 'walks', 'runs', 'skips', 'crawls', 'hops', 'swims', 'jumps', 'climbs'.

Next, ask the children to name another animal and pose a similar range of questions. Ask the children to compare the two animals. *How is their movement the same? How is it different?*

Main Activity

Together, watch videos, DVDs or internet clips that show a variety of animals moving in different ways. Alternatively, share a book about animal movement. Ask the children to describe how the different animals move, including which parts of the body are being used.

Using Resource Sheet 'How Animals Move', identify the animals together and discuss how some of them move. Ask the children to suggest one way of sorting the animals, and together sort a few of the animals using these criteria. Then give each child a copy of the Resource Sheet and a sheet of A3 paper. Ask them to cut out the pictures and to sort the animals into groups according to how they move. They should label each group to show how they have been sorted.

Differentiation: Ask less able children to sort the animals into two groups while more able children could sort the animals into more groups.
Extension: Finishers could add extra animals to each group.

Plenary

Ask the children to explain their groupings to the class. Ask the class to name some animals that don't appear and together place these animals in a group, discussing their reasons.

In a subsequent PE lesson, ask the children to copy the way different animals move.

What to Look For

Children can describe how familiar animals move. They can guess how an unfamiliar animal might move from looking at its picture. They can sort animals into groups which move in a similar way. They can explain why they have sorted the animals in a particular way.

RS

How Animals Move

Eating and Drinking

Science Background

All animals need to eat and drink in order to survive. Water is vital for the functioning of every cell in the body, food is burned as fuel to provide energy for our muscles, and nutrients are extracted from our food that allow our bodies to repair and maintain themselves, and to grow. In Year 1, children should be taught that in order to stay healthy, they need to eat a wide variety of different types of food. They need to know that while all other animals need food and drink, their requirements are different to our own.

Learning Objectives

Children should:

- know that humans and other animals need to eat and drink to stay alive.
- record their ideas about food using drawings and charts.

Resources

- A picture book with a central theme of eating, for example, *I Will Not Ever Never Eat a Tomato* by Lauren Child (Candlewick Press); *Oliver's Vegetables* and *Oliver's Fruit Salad* by Vivian French and Alison Bartlett (Hodder)
- A selection of pet foods for different types of pets
- Plain paper or science books
- Pupil sheet A6 (enlarged to A3 or as an OHT)

Introduction

Share with the children a picture book where eating is a central theme. *Who is the main character in the book? What do they eat? What do you like to eat and drink? Why do we need to eat and drink?* (To get energy, to stay healthy, and to grow.) *What food do we need to eat to stay healthy?* Discuss the fact that people need to eat a variety of different kinds of food. Mention that eating plenty of fruit and vegetables helps you to stay healthy.

Next, show the children the pet food and ask them: *Which pet might eat this food? Which pet might need to eat the most? Which pet might need to eat the least? Why?*

Expand the discussion to include animals that live in the wild, asking: *What do some wild animals eat?* Make sure that examples of carnivores (meat eaters), omnivores (meat and plant eaters) and herbivores (plant eaters) are included in the discussion. Record the children's ideas as a simple chart to provide a model for the Main Activity.

Main Activity

Ask the children to record their ideas about the variety of food that humans and other animals eat on plain paper or in their science books. They can do this through drawings, or a combination of drawing and writing. Encourage them to use the chart (see above) as a starting point for their work. Prompt them to include humans.

Differentiation: More able children could be encouraged to label their pictures and include more animals. Less able children may need support with developing and recording their ideas.

Plenary

Ask the children to tell you the name of an animal from their chart and to give examples of what that animal eats.

Show the children the large copy or OHT of Pupil sheet A6. Read out a riddle and ask the children to identify the correct animal from those illustrated.

What to Look For

Children understand that humans and other animals need food and drink to stay alive, and can identify some foods eaten by humans and other animals in charts or drawings.

Animal Food Riddles

A6

1. I love eating the leaves of any plant. Some people call me a pest because I eat farmers' crops. Cabbages are one of my favourites. Who am I?

2. I spend a lot of time on the ground, looking for insects and earthworms to eat. I also enjoy eating fruit and berries from the trees. Who am I?

3. I make a trap for insects. When they get caught in the trap I gobble them up. Who am I?

4. I eat all sorts of things. I like eating insects, earthworms, berries, wild birds, mice and scraps left by humans. Who am I?

5. I eat small fish and other sea creatures. Who am I?

6. I use poison to help me catch my food. I eat lizards, frogs, baby birds and other small animals. Who am I?

Unit B

Growing Plants

Scientific Enquiry: ● Ask questions and decide how they might find answers to them. ● Explore, using the senses of sight, hearing, smell, touch and taste as appropriate, and make and record observations and measurements. ● Communicate what happened in a variety of ways. ● Compare what happened with what they expected would happen, and try to explain it, drawing on their knowledge and understanding. ● Review their work and explain what they did to others.
Life Processes and Living Things: ● Recognise that plants need light and water to grow. ● Recognise and name the leaf, flower, stem and root of flowering plants. ● Know that seeds grow into flowering plants.
Approximate Teaching Time: 9 hours

Assessment Grid

Unit 1B

	At level 1, children typically:	**At level 2, children typically:**	**At level 3, children typically:**
Life Process and Living Things	● recognise and name the parts of plants. ● communicate observations of a range of plants in terms of features.	● use their knowledge about living things to describe the basic conditions that plants need in order to survive. ● recognise that living things grow and reproduce. ● sort plants into groups, using simple features. ● describe the basis for their groupings. ● recognise that different living things are found in different places.	● use their knowledge and understanding of basic life processes (for example, growth, and reproduction) when they describe differences between living and non-living things. ● provide simple explanations for changes in living things (for example, lack of light or water altering plant growth).

Plants Everywhere

Science Background

Plants are commonly divided into five groups: mosses, ferns, algae, conifers and flowering plants (by far the biggest group). Chlorophyll, the green pigment found in leaves, allows plants to use energy from sunlight to manufacture their own food. Plants are the cornerstone of the planet's ecology. They have played a major part in shaping both landscape and atmosphere, and all animal life depends upon on their existence.

Learning Objectives

Children should:

- know that there are different plants in the immediate environment.
- learn how to treat growing plants with care.
- make and communicate careful observations of one or two plants and where they grow.

Resources

- Adult helpers
- Clipboards and pencils
- A map of the school grounds, including a large copy or transparency
- Camera(s) (preferably digital)
- Computer or interactive whiteboard to display digital photographs
- Pupil sheet B1

Introduction

Ask the children to predict what plants they might find in the school grounds. *Where do you think you will find plants growing? What types of plant do you think you might see?* Record the children's ideas under the headings 'Where?' and 'What?'

Main Activity

Organise the children into small groups, each with an adult. Each child needs a clipboard, a pencil and Pupil sheet B1. Give each adult a map of the school grounds, a clipboard, a pencil and a camera, if available. Explain to the children that they must not touch the plants that they observe for their own safety and the continued wellbeing of the plants.

Ask the adults to take their group around the school grounds looking for plants. When the children find a plant they can identify or they think is particularly interesting, adults should help the children to mark its location on the map. If they cannot name the plant, they should ask the children: *How could we find out the name of this plant?* and prompt them to take a photo or make a detailed, close-up sketch of the plant. Adults should help the children to take photographs of some of the plants. Ensure the adults provide the children with the opportunity to identify a variety of different types of plant, including grasses, weeds and trees.

Plenary

If you have used a digital camera, display some of the photos taken and ask the children to brainstorm words and phrases to describe the plants pictured (for example, 'tall', 'spiky', 'shiny leaves', 'rough bark', etc.). If you have not used a digital camera, do the same using a selection of the sketches.

Ask a child from each group to identify and describe one of the plants that they found, to locate it on the map, and describe where it was growing (for example, in between the paving slabs, in the flower border, at the base of the wall, on the bark of a tree).

Look back at the children's initial ideas, and ask: *Where did you find plants growing? Did you find plants growing in more places than you thought? How many different types of plant did you find? Did you find more types of plants than you thought?*

What to Look For

Children name some plants found around the school and name groups of plants. They describe verbally, by drawing or in simple writing, what the plants are like and where they grow. They recognise when plants should not be pulled up.

⚠ As some plants in the school grounds may be poisonous, irritating to eyes or skin or cause other allergic reactions, caution the children not to touch the plants they observe.

RS

Word Cards for Unit 1B

plants	leaf
leaves	stem
flower	root
seed	water
sprout	seedling
food	healthy
unhealthy	soil
light	grow

Plants Everywhere

B1

Name: ______________________ Date: ______________________

Group: ______________

Name of plant:	Name of plant:
Sketch:	Sketch:
Description:	Description:

Plant Parts

Science Background

Each part of a plant has a specific role to play. The roots have two main functions: they anchor the plant and absorb water from the soil along with trace elements. The leaves are the plant's 'food factory'. They use energy from sunlight and carbon dioxide from the air to carry out photosynthesis. This process produces sugars which the plant needs in order to grow. Plants combine the water they have taken in with the sugars they have made during photosynthesis to form sap, which is circulated around the plant via the stem. Children will learn the names and functions of the various parts of the flower in Key Stage 2. In Key Stage 1 it is sufficient for them to know that flowers are involved in reproduction.

Learning Objectives

Children should:

- know that plants have similar parts.
- know that plants have roots, leaves, stems and flowers.

Resources

- Different varieties of small, flowering plants (in flower); one per table
- Plain paper or science books
- Resource Sheet 'Plant Parts' (enlarged to A3 or as an OHT)

Introduction

Carefully remove one of the flowering plants from the pot and ask the children to name the different parts of the plant (leaves, stem, roots and flowers). As each part is identified, talk with the children in simple terms about what it does (leaves catch the sunlight that the plant needs in order to grow; flowers help to make new plants; roots hold the plant in the soil and suck up water; the stem allows the water to travel to all parts of the plant).

Main Activity

Demonstrate how to add labels to the large copy of Resource Sheet 'Plant Parts'. Ask the children to draw and label a detailed sketch of the plant on their table in their science books or on paper. While they are working, ask individual children to name the different parts of the plants and explain what each part does.

Differentiation: Encourage more able children to annotate their drawing with descriptions of what each part of the plant does.

Plenary

Compare two different plants. Ask, *How are the plants the same?* (same parts: a stem, roots, leaves and flowers) and *How are they different?* (different shape, different size, different shape and/or colour of leaves, different root structure, and different shape and/or colour of flower).

Discuss with the children how they can care for the wellbeing of the plants they have been observing. Explain how to repot the plants and give them some time at the end of the lesson to do this. Ask the children to bring in some food that comes from a plant for the next science lesson.

What to Look For

Children can identify the roots, stem, leaves and flowers of a plant. They make comparisons, identifying differences and some similarities. They communicate their observations in drawings and descriptions.

Plant Parts

RS

stem	root	leaf	flower

Growing Plants

Science Background

Plants play an important role in our daily lives. The majority of our food and drink comes from plant sources. Many materials used in manufacturing are of plant origin, as are a large number of drugs. When a seed germinates, the root grows first and follows the force of gravity downwards. The stem sprouts next, growing against the force of gravity. At first the plant relies on food contained in the seed in order to grow, but once the first leaves form, photosynthesis creates the new material the plant needs to carry on growing.

Learning Objectives

Children should:
- know that plants grow.
- know that plants provide food for humans.
- use drawings to record observations.
- treat growing plants with care.

Resources

- Clear plastic cups with drainage holes (one per child)
- Small drip trays
- Plastic dessert spoons
- Grit
- Potting compost
- Water jugs
- Sticky labels
- Quick-growing 'food seeds' (for example, runner bean, broad bean or sunflower)
- A variety of foods of plant origin brought in by the children (for example, fruit, vegetables, tea, coffee, breakfast cereal, rice, pasta, bread, marmalade, vegetable oil, herbs and spices)
- Pupil sheet B3

Introduction

Ask those children who have brought in a food item to put it on display at the front of the class. Discuss which plant or plants the food comes from.

Main Activity

Tell the children that they will be growing their own 'food plants'. Ask them whether they know what they will need in order to grow a new plant (a seed). Show the different seeds and discuss the similarities and differences between them. Demonstrate how to plant two or three seeds per pot, putting them a couple of centimetres below the surface of the soil and making sure they are next to the wall of the pot so that they can be seen clearly. Explain that seeds need water before they can grow, and show the children how to water the pot. Finally, demonstrate how to label the pots (with the children's names and the type of plant). Organise pairs to plant and label their seeds. Hand each pair a copy of Pupil sheet B3 to keep a record of their plant.

Plenary

How can we care for our seeds now that we have planted them? Discuss the best place to put them (in natural light and out of draughts). Decide who will water them, when and with how much water. If possible, arrange for close adult supervision to prevent over-zealous watering! Ask the children to predict what will happen to their seeds. *How long do you think it will take for your seeds to sprout? What do you think you will you see when they start to sprout?*

Spend a few minutes every other day over the next two weeks looking at the seedlings, discussing changes and recording observations on Pupil sheet B3.

What to Look For

Children state that humans eat some plants and can name some plants that humans eat. Children plant their seeds carefully, following simple instructions. They treat growing plants with care. They use drawings to record their observations.

⚠ Seeds bought from garden centres may have been treated with pesticides. Seeds from health food shops are a safer option.

Growing Plants

B3

Name: ______________________ Date: ______________

Our plant is a ______________________

Week 1	Week 2
Day 1	Day 1
Day 3	Day 3
Day 5	Day 5

Roots

Science Background

The roots of plants have several functions: they anchor the plant in the soil; they absorb water and dissolved minerals from the soil; they may store food, particularly during the winter; and they are involved in the transport of water and dissolved substances (minerals and food sugars) around the plant. There are two main types of root system: the tap root system, where a large primary ('tap') root grows straight down with smaller lateral roots branching off it; and the adventitious (or 'fibrous') root system, where there are numerous roots branching from the stem, all roughly equal in size.

Learning Objectives

Children should:

- to observe and compare the roots of different plants.
- to make careful observations of the plants and to record these in a simple chart or table provided for them.

Resources

- Several plants with large root systems that need repotting (ideally one per table)
- Pots for repotting
- Drip trays
- Grit
- Potting compost
- Water jugs
- Trowels or hand forks
- Several small seedlings (preferably the same species as the larger plants)
- Newspaper
- Computer
- Computer microscope
- Pupil sheet B4

Introduction

Show children the roots of a plant that needs repotting and ask them why they think it needs to be moved to a bigger pot. Compare the roots with those of some seedlings. Encourage the children to describe the similarities and differences between the two root systems with reference to the colour, thickness, length and complexity of the roots. Demonstrate how to repot the plants.

Main Activity

On each table put a plant with a large root system that needs repotting and at least one seedling (preferably of the same type as the larger plant). Ask the children to remove the plants from their pots and draw detailed sketches of the two root systems on Pupil sheet B4. Arrange for one pair at a time to use the computer microscope (under adult supervision) to look at the roots of the large plant and the seedling and to record their observations on the Pupil sheet (either by printing out the image and sticking it on, or by drawing). When it is time to clear away, ask the children to put the seedlings back in their pots and repot the bigger plants.

Differentiation: More able children could write descriptive words and phrases in the space around each drawing (for example, 'white', 'long', 'thin', 'hairy', 'jumbled up', 'wiggly' etc.).

Plenary

How do a plant's roots change as it gets bigger? (They get longer, thicker and there are more of them.) *Why do you think this happens?* (A larger plant needs more water and support.)

Show the children some seedlings that have been left to dry out and are starting to wilt. *Do these plants look healthy? What should a healthy plant look like? What's wrong with them? What can we do to help them recover?* If no one suggests that they need water, ask one child to feel the soil. Help the children to plan a test in which some plants are watered and some are not. Ask the children what they think will happen. Give the plants their first drink of water and, later in the day, check their progress.

What to Look For

The children can identify the roots of a plant. They make comparisons between the roots of a larger and smaller plant, identifying differences and similarities. They communicate their observations in drawings and with verbal descriptions.

Roots

B4

Name: ____________________ Date: ____________________

Roots of a large plant:	Roots of a seedling:
Roots of a large plant seen through the microscope:	Roots of a seedling seen through the microscope:

The Light Stuff

Science Background

While animals rely on the food they eat to provide them with energy, plants take their energy directly from the sun. They use solar energy to convert water and carbon dioxide into sugar and oxygen. They cannot use the oxygen and so they release it into the air as a waste product. If a plant grows in an area of uneven lighting, it will lean to face towards the light in order to maximise the amount of light reaching the leaves. (**Note**: This lesson consists of a short initial session of 30 minutes and four additional ten-minute slots over the course of two weeks.)

Learning Objectives

Children should:

- know that green plants need light to grow.
- turn ideas about whether green plants need light to grow into a form that can be tested.
- know that plants are living but that an artificial plant is not living.
- observe and compare green plants grown in light and dark places.
- conclude that green plants need light to grow well.

Resources

- Two plants that are very different to each other
- Two identical plants
- Two containers or jugs full of water: one very small; one very large
- An artificial pot plant and its living counterpart
- Two card labels reading 'living' and two 'not living'
- Pupil sheet B5

Introduction

What do plants need to grow? (Water and light) If the children are slow to respond, remind them about the watering experiment from the previous lesson. Once someone mentions light, ask: *How can we test whether plants need light to grow?* Take suggestions from the children about how you might set up and carry out the test, and what you will observe.

Main Activity

Set up the test in front of the children, asking them to watch very carefully to make sure the test is fair. Make the following errors: start with two completely different types of plant; suggest putting one in the fridge; use a huge jug to water one plant and a tiny jug to water the other. As you set up the test, talk about what you are doing. If no one spots your deliberate mistakes, draw the children's attention to them by saying, for example: *Hmm, I'm not sure that starting with two different types of plant is very fair.* Once it has been established that something you are doing is unfair, ask the children: *What can I do to make it fair?* Once the test is set up, ask the children to predict what they think will happen and why.

Observe the plants at regular intervals over the next two weeks. Each time, ask the children to describe the differences between the plant in the dark and the plant in the light. Ask them to predict what they think the differences will be the next time they look at the plants. During the final observation ask the children to complete a copy of Pupil sheet B5. They should draw a sketch of each plant and write words to describe it. A word list is given at the bottom of the page to help them.

Plenary

Display an artificial plant and a very similar real plant side by side. Ask the children to label them 'living' or 'not living' using the prepared card labels. Then ask them to explain how they know that one is living and the other is not. Introduce a real plant that has died and ask the children to label it and justify their classification. Finally ask: *Why do you think this plant died?* (Probably not enough water or light.)

What to Look For

Children suggest a way of finding out whether green plants need light to grow. They identify differences between the plant kept in the dark and the plant kept in the light. They can draw a conclusion from the results, for example: 'I think that plants need light because the one that was kept in the dark didn't look healthy.'

Do Plants Need Light to Grow?

B5

Name: ____________________ Date: ____________________

This plant was kept in the **light**.	This plant was kept in the **dark**.
Draw it here:	Draw it here:
Write about it here:	Write about it here:

healthy	unhealthy	green
not green	droopy	firm
bushy	straggly	alive
dead	large	small

What Do We Know About Plants?

Science Background

This lesson offers an opportunity to assess the children's individual understanding of the work covered in this unit.

Learning Objectives

Children should:

- demonstrate their understanding of Unit 1B.

Resources

- Blank book (big book if available) entitled *Our Big Book of Plants* (or similar)
- An infant non-fiction book in big book format (any subject)
- Pupil sheet B6 (enlarged to A3 or as an OHT)
- Unlabelled pictures of familiar plants

Introduction

Explain to the children that they are going to make a book about plants for the children in Reception. Show them the blank book that you have prepared. Explain that because the children in Reception class cannot read very well yet, most of the information in the book will need to be in the form of pictures.

Main Activity

Show the children the display copy of Pupil sheet B6 and the unlabelled pictures of familiar plants. Explain that you would like them to choose one plant and write its name in the top box of their Pupil sheet. They will then draw a picture of it in the large box in the middle of the sheet. Remind pupils to include the part of the plant that grows under the ground (even though this may not be shown on the pictures they are working from). Explain that the four smaller boxes either side of the picture are for labels identifying the different parts of the plant. Show the children where they will write what the different parts of a plant do and draw a picture showing what a plant needs to grow and stay healthy. Finally, ask them to write their name in the small box on the bottom right.

Give each child their own copy of the Pupil sheet and a copy of the pictures of familiar plants to complete the activity as described.

To ensure that this lesson is a true assessment of what the children know, the assistance you provide should be limited. Remind the children about what they have to do, and help them to place their work in the correct boxes but do not help with ideas. Only give spelling help as requested rather than providing a word list. Encourage every child to work on their own. Do not provide access to any written reference materials.

Extension: Ask children who finish this task to write anything else they know about the plant they have drawn on another piece of paper (for example, where it grows or what it is used for).

Plenary

Show some of the work produced and ask children to elaborate on their drawings.

After the lesson, help a small group to organise the book into chapters and add a contents page and an index. Children who are able readers might like to prepare a glossary. Once the book is finished, allow the children some time to read it before taking it to the Reception class. When the Reception class have finished with the book, keep it as a permanent record of assessment for Unit 1B.

What to Look For

Children name some common plants. They can identify the leaf, root, stem and flower of a plant. They recognise that plants are living and need water and light to grow.

Our Big Book of Plants

B6

Name: ______________________ Date: ______________

My plant:

What to the different parts of a plant do?

What does a plant need to grow and stay healthy?

Unit C

Sorting and Using Materials

Scientific Enquiry: • Recognise the importance of collecting evidence by making observations and measurements when trying to answer a question. • Ask questions and decide how they might find answers to them. • Explore, using the senses of sight, hearing, smell, touch and taste as appropriate, and make and record observations and measurements. • Communicate what happened in a variety of ways.
Materials and Their Properties: • Use their senses to explore and recognise the similarities and differences between materials. • Sort objects into groups on the basis of simple material properties. • Recognise and name common types of material. • Find out about the uses of a variety of materials and how these are chosen for specific uses on the basis of their simple properties.
Approximate Teaching Time: 9 hours

Assessment Grid

Unit 1C

	At level 1, children typically:	**At level 2, children typically:**	**At level 3, children typically:**
Materials and Their Properties	• know about a range of properties (for example, texture and appearance) and communicate observations of materials in terms of these properties.	• identify a range of common materials and know about some of their properties. • describe similarities and differences between materials. • sort materials into groups and describe the basis for their groupings in everyday terms (for example, shininess, hardness, smoothness).	• use their knowledge and understanding of materials when they describe a variety of ways of sorting them into groups according to their properties. • explain simply why some materials are particularly suitable for specific purposes.

Exploring Materials

Science Background

Elastic objects revert back to their original shape when the force that is distorting them is removed (for example, a rubber band, a ruler or a sponge). Plastic objects, however, are mouldable and stay in the shape they have been moulded into (for example, modelling clay, wet sand, aluminium foil).

Learning Objectives

Children should:

- know that every material has many properties which can be recognised using our senses and described using appropriate vocabulary.
- record observations of materials.

Resources

- A collection of about 12 objects for each table (for example, a sponge, play dough, a teaspoon, a wooden spoon, aluminium foil, a ruler, a cork, a twig, a maraca, scented paper, a pine cone, sandpaper)
- An interesting object, for example a pumice
- Plain paper or science books
- A tray of six everyday objects (for example, a matchbox containing a few spent matches, a bar of soap, a hairbrush, a tea bag, a drinks can from the fridge, a scented fruit)
- Blindfold
- Pupil sheet C1

Introduction

Show the children your interesting or unusual object and draw a picture of it on the board. Ask the following questions and write each answer around the drawing. (For the questions that involve using the senses, ask one child to come up to feel or smell the object.) *Is it shiny or dull? Is it rough or smooth? Is it bendy or stiff? Is it soft or hard? Is it warm or cool to touch? Can you change its shape? Does it make a noise when you shake it? Does it smell?*

Review the descriptions and ask the children to tell you the sense or senses they used to find the answer.

Main Activity

Children repeat the activity at their tables, choosing one object at a time from a selection, drawing a detailed picture of it in the centre of a page in their science books or on a piece of paper and writing descriptive words and phrases around their drawing.

Differentiation: For most children, provide a copy of the word list on Pupil sheet C1. However, more able writers could write independently.

As they work, explore with the children the distinction between objects that are bendy, stretchy or squashy (elastic), and those that change their shape (plastic) – see Science Background, above.

Plenary

Play a game of 'Guess the Object'. Blindfold a volunteer and let them handle one object from the tray. Ask them to guess what the object is. Ask the class which sense the volunteer cannot use (sight) and which other senses they will have to rely on to help them identify the object (touch, smell and hearing). Encourage the other children to ask the blindfolded child questions about what they can feel, hear and smell (for example: *Is it rough or smooth? Can you bend it? Is it soft or hard? Does it make a noise if you shake it?).* Finally, ask the volunteer to tell the class what they think the object is and why, referring to how the object feels, smells or sounds. Repeat the process with a new volunteer and a different object.

What to Look For

Children use a variety of appropriate words to describe materials and objects. They describe how objects and materials look, feel, smell and sound. They record their observations through annotated drawings. They ask suitable questions that enable others to describe objects. They understand the difference between an object that is bendy, stretchy or squashy and one that changes shape.

RS

Word Cards for Unit 1C

material	shiny
dull	rough
smooth	bendy
stiff	soft
hard	wood
metal	plastic
glass	mixture
magnetic	waterproof

Exploring Materials

C1

Name: ______________________ Date: ______________

	dull		shiny
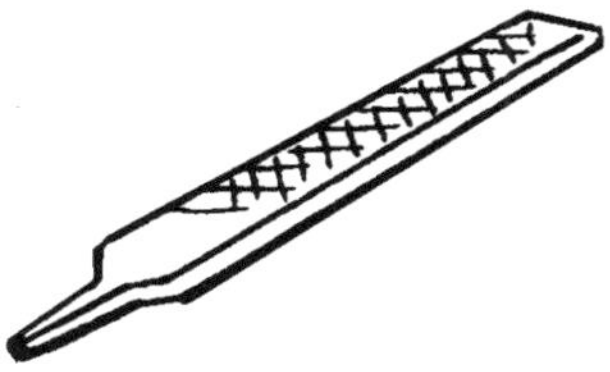	rough	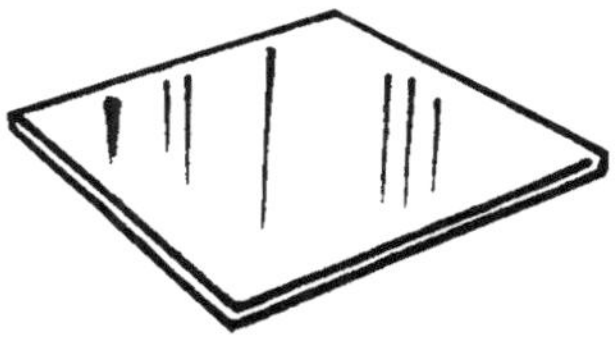	smooth
	hard		soft
	cool		warm
	bendy stretchy squashy	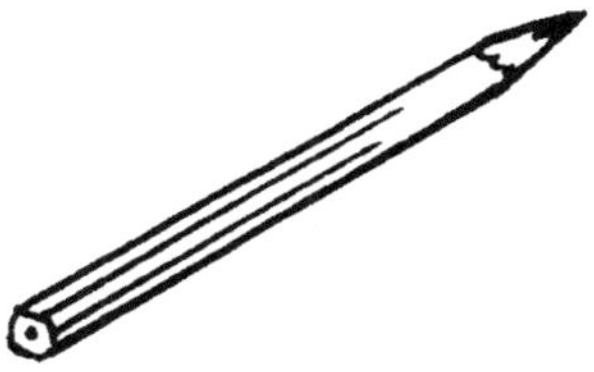	stiff
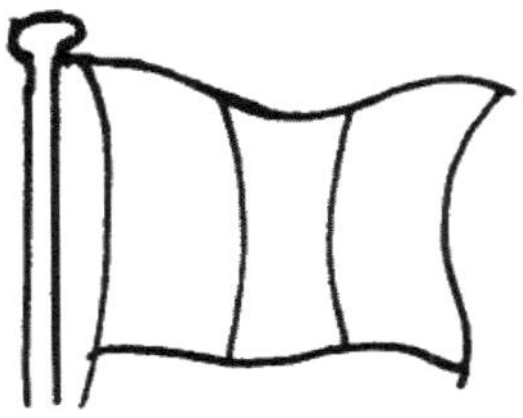	can change shape	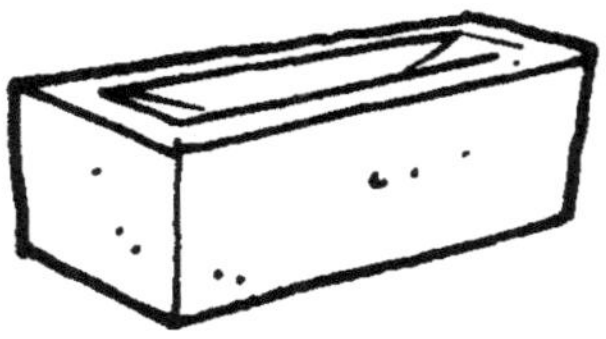	can't change shape
	makes a noise		doesn't make a noise
	smells		doesn't smell

Identifying Materials

Science Background

Children often confuse the scientific term 'material' with the more general meaning of the word, 'fabric'. Use the word repeatedly in a scientific context to help the children become familiar with this 'new' meaning (for example, ask: *What material is this made from?* rather than *What is this made from?*). Children can also confuse the name of an object and the material it is made from, especially when both words are the same (for example, 'brick'). If a child names an object rather than the material, repeat the question: *What material is it made from?*

Learning Objectives

Children should:

- know that there are many different materials which can be named and described.
- know that objects are made from materials.
- know that different objects can be made from the same materials.

Resources

- A box of about 12 everyday objects made from wood, metal, plastic, glass and a mixture of these materials. Include some materials which have not been made into artefacts (for example, a lump of wood, a piece of sheet metal).
- Five hoops labelled 'wood', 'metal', 'plastic', 'glass' and 'a mixture of materials'
- Adult helpers, if available
- Clipboards and pencils
- Reference books about materials
- Pupil sheet C2

Introduction

Put the hoops on the floor and ask the class to sit around them. Tell the children that today you will be looking at what things are made from, and introduce the term 'material'. Ask a child to pick out an object from the box, and ask them: *Which material is this made from?* As the materials are correctly identified, ask the child to put the object they chose into the correct hoop. If the object is a mixture of materials, discuss which materials it is a mixture of. When all the objects have been sorted, ask the children to describe the characteristics of each material. Ask, for example: *What are the metal objects like?* (Quite shiny, cool to touch, often a silvery colour.)

Main Activity

Take the children on a 'materials hunt' around the school, recording objects that are made from wood, metal, plastic and glass. If you have adult helpers, each group could go to a different area of the school. Children should record their observations in the form of notes or labelled drawings on Pupil sheet C2.

Back in the classroom, use reference books to find out more about each material and where we get it from (wood is cut from trees, plastic is manufactured from petroleum oil, metal is extracted from special sorts of rock called 'ores', and glass is produced by heating a mixture of sand, soda and lime to very high temperatures).

Plenary

Bring the children's attention to the 'any other material' box at the bottom of their Pupil sheet. Ask them to describe the objects they found that were made from materials other than wood, metal, plastic or glass. Together identify the materials that these objects are made from (for example, paths are made from concrete, bricks are made from brick, tiles are made from clay or slate). Talk about other materials that might be found in the classroom and ask the children to suggest examples of these (for example, books are made from paper).

What to Look For

Children can name and describe several common materials. They can identify different objects made of the same material and name the material.

Materials Hunt

C2

Name: ____________________ Date: ____________________

wood	metal
plastic	glass
any other material	a mixture of materials

Sorting Materials

Science Background

The essential concepts underlying this lesson are that every material possesses a variety of properties, and that these properties can provide criteria for putting it into a group with other materials. It is important that children appreciate that there are many ways of sorting materials, which are all equally valid.

Learning Objectives

Children should:

- group materials together and make a record of groupings.
- know that materials can be sorted in a variety of ways according to their properties.
- use appropriate vocabulary to describe materials.

Resources

- For each table, an identical collection of about 12 different papers, cards and other materials that are fairly flat and can be stuck down easily (for example, coloured Cellophane, aluminium foil, tracing paper, sugar paper, textured wallpaper, sandpaper, gummed paper, scented paper, corrugated cardboard, thin card, paper doily, paper towel)
- A different collection of about six similar materials (for example, baking parchment, bubble wrap, plastic cut from a file pocket, shiny paper, crêpe paper and tissue paper)
- Scissors
- Glue sticks
- Sorting hoops
- Pupil sheet C3 enlarged to A3

Introduction

Ask the children to identify the small collection of materials in turn, asking them to identify the material and then to suggest words to describe it. Then draw two large circles on the board. Explain to the class that you are going to sort the materials into two groups and that you want them to guess how you have sorted them (for example, rough and smooth). Repeat the game, sorting the materials according to different criteria (for example, see-through and not see-through). Finally, ask a child to lead the game, sorting the materials in a third way (for example, shiny and dull, brown and not brown). Explain that everyone will now play the same game working together as a team on their table.

Main Activity

Provide each table with an identical collection of materials and two hoops. Allow the children a few minutes to sort the materials on their table into two sets. (Encourage them to work quietly.) When all the groups have finished, allow the children five minutes to look at the sorted materials on the other tables. Finally, walk the whole class around the room one table at a time. Look at the materials on each table and ask: *How have these materials been sorted? What are all the materials in this hoop like? What labels could we put on each hoop?* Ask the children who worked on each table to confirm whether these ideas are correct.

Explain to the children that they are now going to sort the materials on their own, and record their groupings. Demonstrate how to do this with an enlarged copy of Pupil sheet C3. Label each circle and ask the children to stick a small piece of each material in the appropriate circle. Give each child an enlarged copy of the Pupil sheet to work with. While the children are working, talk to individuals about how they are grouping their materials and ask them to suggest as many words as they can to describe one or more of the materials.

Plenary

Ask volunteers to show their work and explain how they have sorted the materials. Record each new sorting method on the board (for example, dull or shiny). *How many different ways have we found of sorting the materials?* If appropriate, ask: *Can anyone think of any more ways that we could have sorted them?*

What to Look For

Children identify and name properties of materials and sort materials into groups on the basis of these. They record their groupings. They can identify a common characteristic in a group of materials sorted by someone else.

C3

Sorting Materials

Name: ______________________ Date: ______________________

Choosing Materials

Science Background

Different materials are chosen for different purposes, depending on the properties they possess. Some of the most important considerations when choosing materials for manufacturing are hardness (resistance to changing shape); toughness (the ability to absorb energy without shattering); strength (resistance to breaking when a force is applied); flexibility (the ability to bend easily without breaking) and elasticity (the ability to return to the original shape after a force has been applied). Materials' properties depend on the structure of their molecules. Diamond, for example, consists purely of the element carbon. The carbon atoms are arranged in a regular structure and each atom is joined to four others. Graphite is also made entirely of carbon but it has a different molecular structure, giving it different properties.

Learning Objectives

Children should:

- know that materials can be used in a variety of ways.
- use appropriate vocabulary to describe materials.
- suggest how to test an idea about whether a fabric or paper is suitable for a particular purpose.

Resources

- Number fans (numbered at least 1–8)
- A display of the following materials – numbered from 1 to 8: cotton wool; steel wool; acetate; a straight piece of rigid, smooth plastic or wood; cardboard; a cloth; newspaper; a cork
- A selection of six different wrapping materials (papers, cards and fabrics)
- One parcel wrapped in parcel paper, one that is unwrapped
- Pupil sheet C4

Introduction

Display the materials listed in Resources, labelled 1 to 8. Ask the class the following questions: *Which material would you use for making the windows on a doll's house? Getting mud off your bike? Cleaning the oven? Making a model fort? Padding a packing crate when you move house? Making a bed for a hamster? Making a ramp for toy cars? Making a model raft?* The children should decide which is the best material each time, then hold up the appropriate number on their number fan. Sometimes more than one answer may be acceptable. After each answer is given, ask the children to justify their choices, referring to the properties of the materials.

Main Activity

Show the children the wrapped and unwrapped packages. Explain that you want to send them both through the post but that you have run out of parcel paper. Ask the class to help you choose an alternative from a selection of different wrapping materials. *What will the material I use to wrap the parcel need to be like?* (Strong, easy to fold and easy to write on.) Divide the class into three groups and assign each group a different characteristic to test. The three groups can be further divided into smaller groups, each with the same selection of materials to test. Discuss the children's ideas about how they will test the materials.

Differentiation: Less able children may need support deciding how to carry out their test.
Extension: Children record their test results and order the materials on Pupil sheet C4.

Plenary

Ask each group: *What were you trying to find out about the materials? What did you do to test them? Which material do you think I should wrap the parcel with?* Note each group's recommendation and, finally, discuss with the children the need to make a compromise (for example, the strongest material may not be the easiest to fold; the easiest material to write on may not be very strong). Help the children to identify the material that performs best across all three categories.

What to Look For

Children identify and name properties of materials. They suggest what paper for wrapping a parcel should be like. They suggest an appropriate way of testing the papers for the chosen characteristic and carry out their test.

Wrapping a Parcel

C4

Name: ____________________ Date: ____________

- Tick one box.

We have tested

- ☐ how strong
- ☐ how easy to fold
- ☐ how easy to write on

the materials are.

This is what we did.

This is how we have ordered the materials.

Best

1. ____________________
2. ____________________
3. ____________________
4. ____________________
5. ____________________
6. ____________________

Worst

Magnetic Materials

Science Background

Magnetic materials are used in a wide range of engineering applications. They are essential in the creation and distribution of electricity. They are also an important component in many electrical appliances, including PCs, CD players, televisions, games consoles and loudspeakers. They are used to store data on floppy disks, audio and video tapes. If a material is easily magnetised and demagnetised, then it is referred to as a 'soft' magnetic material. If it is difficult to demagnetise, then it is referred to as a 'hard' (or permanent) magnetic material.

Learning Objectives

Children should:

- know that some materials are magnetic but most are not.
- know that some metals are magnetic, but nothing that is not a metal is magnetic.
- think about which objects they expect to be attracted to a magnet.
- make observations and communicate what happened.
- with help, use results to draw conclusions, saying whether their predictions were correct.

Resources

- A variety of different types of magnet: bar, horseshoe, magnetic letters, fridge magnets, etc.
- Enough bar or horseshoe magnets for one between two
- Boxes (one per table) containing a variety of small objects to test, both magnetic and non-magnetic
- A different collection of about ten objects, some magnetic, some not
- Coloured pencils
- Pupil sheet C5, enlarged to A3

Introduction

Provide each table with a selection of different magnets and a box of objects, and allow the children between five and ten minutes to experiment with these. Don't give them any guidance – just tell them that at the end of the activity you will be asking them to tell you something about the magnets. As the children play, talk to individuals about what they are doing and ask them what they have found out about the magnets.

At the end of the session, remove the magnets from the tables, gather the children together, and ask them to tell you what they have found out.

Main Activity

Draw two circles on the board, label one 'magnetic' and the other 'not magnetic', and explain these terms. Show the class four or five objects, identify which materials they are made from and ask the class to predict whether the object will be attracted to a magnet or not. Draw the objects in the appropriate circle. Now ask a child to test the first object with a magnet. Record the results by drawing pictures in the appropriate circles in a different colour to the predictions. Repeat with all the objects. *Which objects are magnetic? Which objects are not magnetic? Were your predictions right?*

Organise pairs to carry out the same test at their tables, using the objects in their box. Provide each pair with Pupil sheet C5. Hand out the bar or horseshoe magnets only when that group's predictions are complete.

Plenary

Which objects are magnetic? Which are not magnetic? Were your predictions right? Then ask, *Which materials are magnetic?* (Some metals) *Was anything that wasn't a metal magnetic?* (No) Ask the children to predict whether further objects are magnetic, giving explanations for their predictions (for example, 'It looks like it's made out of metal, so it might be magnetic' or, 'It's not made out of metal, so it can't be magnetic'). Ask the children to suggest some everyday uses of magnets (for example, fridge magnets, noticeboard magnets, door closures, fishing games).

What to Look For

Children identify some objects that are attracted to a magnet. They predict which objects will be attracted to a magnet and say whether they were right. They recognise that objects that are attracted to magnets are made of metal but that not all metal objects are attracted.

Magnetic or Not?

C5

Name: ______________________________ Date: ______________________

✓	magnetic

✗	not magnetic

Colour key

our predictions ☐

our results ☐

Is It Waterproof?

Science Background

Materials are described as waterproof if they do not allow water to pass through them. Absorbent fabrics can be 'proofed' to make them resistant to water. The proofing process usually involves applying a liquid on one or both sides of the material which then dries to form an impermeable layer. For example, rubber dissolved in naphtha was used by the industrialist Charles Macintosh, who not only gave his name to the process, but also the garment most commonly made from his treated fabric.

Learning Objectives

Children should:

- suggest how to test whether materials are waterproof.
- explore ways of answering the question.
- communicate what they did and what happened, making simple comparisons.
- use what happened to draw a conclusion and to say what they found out.

Resources

- Barnaby Bear or similar soft toy
- For each table, the same selection of fabrics and other foldable materials, some waterproof and some not
- Plastic teaspoons
- Water pots
- Paper towels for spillages
- Pupil sheet C6

Introduction

Explain that Barnaby Bear has lost his rain hat. He needs to make himself another one, but he doesn't know what material to make it from. *How could you help Barnaby to find a suitable material for his rain hat? What would the material need to be like?* (Waterproof) Show the children the materials they will be testing. *How could we find out which materials are waterproof?* Discuss the children's ideas. They might suggest they pour water into the middle of the material then look under it to find out whether there is any water on the table. If so, prompt them to think about how they will prevent water from spilling over the edge of the material (for example, by using a fairly large piece of material and lifting up the corners to form a 'bag' shape). *Which materials do you think will be waterproof? Why?* Record the children's predictions in a simple two-column table, labelled 'waterproof' and 'not waterproof'.

Main Activity

Children carry out their investigation in small groups. As they test each material, they should sort them into two piles – one waterproof and one not. Once they have finished the test they should record their groupings using drawings, words, or a combination of both, on Pupil sheet C6.

Differentiation: Ask more able children to order the materials in their 'not waterproof' pile according to how much water they let through.

Plenary

Ask one child from each group to explain how they carried out their test. *Which materials are waterproof? How do you know?* (They didn't let the water through.) *Which materials aren't waterproof? How do you know?* (They let water through.) *Which materials would be a good choice for making Barnaby's hat? Why?* (… because they're waterproof and the others aren't.) *Which would be the worst choice for Barnaby's hat? Why?* (… because it let the most water through.) *Were your predictions right?* In further sessions, small groups could work with an adult to make Barnaby a hat from one of the waterproof materials that they identified.

What to Look For

The children recognise that a rain hat needs to be waterproof. They find a way to decide whether a material is waterproof and describe this to others. They use their results to group materials.

Is It Waterproof?

C6

Name: ____________________ Date: ____________________

waterproof	not waterproof

Unit D

Light and Dark

Scientific Enquiry: ● Ask questions and decide how they might find answers to them. ● Explore, using the senses of sight, hearing, smell, touch and taste as appropriate, and make and record observations and measurements. ● Communicate what happened in a variety of ways. ● Make simple comparisons and identify simple patterns or associations. ● Compare what happened with what they expected would happen, and try to explain it, drawing on their knowledge and understanding. ● Review their work and explain what they did to others.
Life Processes and Living Things: ● Know about the senses that enable humans and other animals to be aware of the world around them.
Physical Processes: ● Identify different light sources, including the Sun. ● Understand that dakrness is the absence of light.
Approximate Teaching Time: 6 hours

Assessment Grid

Unit 1D

	At level 1, children typically:	**At level 2, children typically:**	**At level 3, children typically:**
Physical Processes	• communicate observations of changes in light that result from actions. • recognise that light comes from a variety of sources and name some of these.	• know about a range of physical phenomena and recognise and describe similarities and differences associated with them. • compare the brightness or colour of lights.	• use their knowledge and understanding of physical phenomena to link *cause* and *effect* in simple explanations. • begin to make simple generalisations about physical phenomena.

Light Sources

Science Background

Light sources give out light, which travels from the source in straight lines. When light hits an object, some of it is absorbed and some of it is reflected. Dull objects reflect the least light, while shiny objects reflect the most. Children can find it difficult to distinguish between true light sources and shiny objects (which reflect light from another source). This idea is reinforced in Lesson 4.

Learning Objectives

Children should:

- know that there are many sources of light.
- make comparisons between light sources in terms of brightness or colour.
- know that sources of light show up best at night-time.

Resources

- Story book where darkness is a theme, for example, *The Owl Who Was Afraid of the Dark* by Jill Tomlinson (Mammoth)
- A collection of different light sources (for example, pocket torch, tea light, gas lighter, table lamp, head torch)
- Matches (to light the tea light)
- Adult helpers, if available
- Clipboards, paper and pencils
- Resource Sheet 'Is it a Light Source?' (enlarged to A3 or as an OHT)

Introduction

Introduce the topic by reading the story book and discussing with the children their own feelings about the dark. *Are you afraid of the dark sometimes? What can you do to feel better when you're frightened of the dark?* Explain that darkness is merely the absence of light. Tell the children that in science this half term they will be learning about light.

Main Activity

Explain that something that gives out light is called a light source. Show the children your collection of light sources and demonstrate how they give out light. Ask children to compare the light from the different sources (for example, 'This one is the brightest', 'That one is dimmer than this one', 'They're different colours').

Take the children (with adult helpers, if available) on a walk around the school, looking for sources of light. Ask pairs to record all the sources of light that they find. As they work, ask the children to describe the differences and similarities between the various light sources.

Back in the classroom, ask the children to suggest light sources they use on special occasions (for example, Christmas tree lights, bonfires and fireworks, Hallowe'en lanterns, and Divali lights). Ask the children what time of day most of these are used and why (for example, firework displays take place at night when it is dark so they can be seen better). Ask the children (in the same pairs as earlier) to draw as many different light sources as they can to add to their collection of light sources from the walk.

Plenary

Play a light source game, using a large copy or transparency of Resource Sheet 'Is it a Light Source?' Ask the children whether they think each picture shows a light source or not. Explain that some things (for example, the moon, a mirror, a diamond ring, aluminium foil) do not give out light themselves, but reflect the light coming from another source.

What to Look For

Children identify a number of light sources of different kinds and make comparisons between light sources in terms of brightness or colour. They understand that light sources show up best in the dark.

⚠ Keep the matches away from the children and make sure that the tea light is not left burning unattended.

RS

Word Cards for Unit 1D

light	dark
darkness	source
brighter	dimmer
night	day
bright	clouds
the Sun	shadow
dull	shiny
reflect	reflective

Is It a Light Source?

RS

traffic lights	

lightning	

clouds	

the stars	

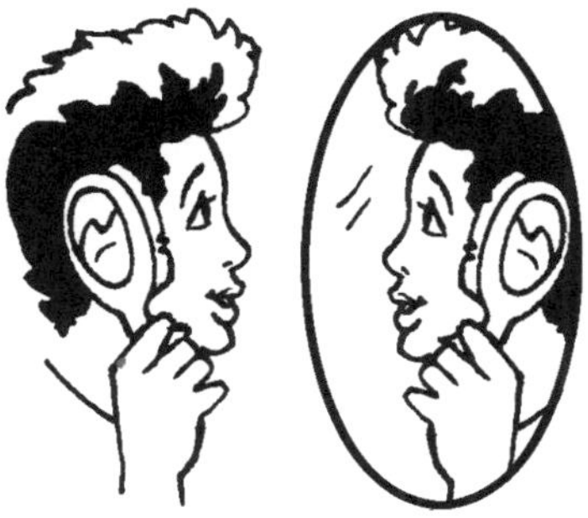

a mirror	

the Moon	

aluminium foil	

hairdryer	

diamond ring	

pebble	

the Sun	

tree	

The Sun

Science Background

The Sun is a star, approximately 1.39 million km in diameter. The central powerhouse of our solar system, its gravitational pull keeps all the planets in motion and it is the ultimate source of all our energy. The Earth orbits the Sun in an elliptical orbit, at an average distance of 150 million km. As it orbits it also spins in an anticlockwise direction, one revolution every 24 hours, and it is this spin that creates day and night. One common misconception among children at this age is that the Sun moves around the Earth.

Learning Objectives

Children should:

- know that the Sun is the source of light for the Earth.
- know that it is dangerous to look at the Sun because it is so bright.
- make observations and to try to explain these.

Resources

- Darkened classroom
- Powerful torch
- Globe
- Alternatively, go to the 'day and night' section on www.schoolsobservatory.org.uk for an animation called 'spinning globe'. The globe goes very fast if you run it at the set speed, so don't press the play button, but drag the progress bar manually.
- A set of photographs, some taken on a dull day, some on a sunny day and some at night
- Pupil sheet D2

Introduction

First make sure that all the lights in the classroom are switched off. Briefly recap work on light sources covered in the previous session. *Is it light or dark right now?* Ask the children to tell you where the light is coming from. *Where is the Sun on a sunny day? Where is the Sun on a dull day?*

Main Activity

On a sunny day with some clouds, take the children outside. Warn them never to look directly at the Sun as it is so bright that it can blind them. Ask them how else they might discover whether the Sun is 'out' or not without looking at it. Develop the idea of looking for shadows (the children's own or those of objects in the playground). Ask the children to tell you when the Sun is covered by clouds and when there are no clouds covering the Sun. Avoid the use of language that suggests that the Sun itself is moving (for example, don't say: *The Sun has gone behind a cloud*). Ask the children to explain how they can tell whether a cloud is covering the Sun. *When a cloud covers the Sun, is the Sun still our source of light?* (Yes)

Back in the classroom, ask the children to explain how they think day and night occur. *What happens to the Sun at night-time?* Once you have collected their ideas, either run the 'spinning globe' animation (see Resources), or use the globe and torch to demonstrate how the Earth's spin causes day and night. Draw the children's attention to the fact that the Sun is constantly shining on the Earth, and that night-time happens when our part of the Earth is facing away from the Sun. Read through Pupil sheet D2 with the children then ask them to complete it individually.

Differentiation: Less able readers might need support in this activity.
Extension: More able children could also draw a labelled diagram showing how day and night occur.

Plenary

Show the children a set of photographs taken on a dull day, on a sunny day and at night, and ask them to sort them into three sets. Invite them to explain the reasons why they have sorted them in the way they have. Encourage them to tell you where the Sun was when each set of photographs was taken.

What to Look For

Children identify changes that occur when the Sun is covered by a cloud and recognise that these are different from changes at nightfall. They explain that the Sun is a source of light even when it is behind a cloud.

They can explain why it is dangerous to look directly at the Sun.

⚠ Warn children never to look directly at the Sun.

The Sun

D2

Name: ______________________ Date: ______________________

- Tick one square and one circle in each question to show the right answer.

1.

When there are no clouds covering the Sun

it is ☐ bright ☐ dark ☐ dull

and there are ◯ shadows ◯ no shadows.

2.

When clouds cover the Sun

it is ☐ bright ☐ dark ☐ dull

and there are ◯ shadows ◯ no shadows.

3.

At night-time

it is ☐ bright ☐ dark ☐ dull

and there are ◯ shadows ◯ no shadows.

Can You See in the Dark?

Science Background

It is essential that the 'dark area' used in Group Activity 1 below is as close to total darkness as possible. One of the quickest and most reliable ways of achieving this is by draping blackout material over a pre-existing framework, such as a playhouse. Blackout material can be bought by the metre from photographic specialists.

Learning Objectives

Children should:

- know that light is essential for seeing things.
- know that when it is dark other senses can be used to help us find and identify things.
- observe and make comparisons of sources of light and to try to explain what they observed.

Resources

- A 'dark area' in a corner of the classroom (see Science Background above)
- Two 'black' boxes (a cardboard box with a tiny peephole in one end and a larger, covered hole in the top)
- Two 'mystery objects' to go inside the black boxes
- A range of different torches, two of each
- Day and night photographs of the same scene
- Magazines and catalogues
- Scissors
- Glue sticks
- Large pieces of sugar paper
- Three adult helpers

Introduction

Divide the class into three groups. Assign two adults to Activity 1 and one adult each to Activities 2 and 3. Spend between ten and 15 minutes on each activity before moving around.

Main Activity

Group Activity 1: Ask the children to make a group collage of sources of light by cutting and sticking images from magazines and catalogues. Once they are busy, take two children at a time into the dark area. Ask one child to find the other and to describe what they are doing, for example, 'I'm putting my hands out in front of me and feeling along the floor.' When they have found each other ask: *Which sense would you normally use to find her?* (Sight) *Why can't you use sight now? Which other senses were you using to help you find her?* (Touch and hearing) Repeat the activity with the other child doing the finding. Finally, increase light levels gradually. Ask the children to tell you when they can see each other easily and explain why this is.

Group Activity 2: Divide this group into two smaller groups and give each a 'black box'. Ask the children to find out whether they can see the mystery object inside the box when there is no light (i.e. when the top hole is covered). Provide a variety of torches and ask the children to shine light into the top hole to find out what is in the box. Ask them to describe when the object was easiest to see.

Group Activity 3: Show the children a photograph taken during the day and the same scene by night. Discuss the differences between the two pictures. *How many sources of light can you see in each picture? Which colours can you see in each picture? What can you see in the night-time picture? Can you see things in the daytime picture that you cannot see in the night picture?* Ask the children to explain the reasons behind their observations.

Plenary

Start a discussion by asking the children: *Can you see in the dark?* Explain that in total darkness you cannot see at all, and that introducing more light allows you to see more clearly. Discuss the ways in which the world looks different at night-time compared with during the day.

What to Look For

Children describe how they try to find something when it is dark and recognise they cannot use their sense of sight in the dark. They state that they can see things when there is some light. They recognise that a torch will enable an object in a 'black box' to be seen but that when there is no light they cannot see the object. They recognise that some torches give brighter light than others and explain that objects are easier to see in brighter light.

Being Seen at Night

Science Background

Many local councils run an annual 'Be Safe, Be Seen' campaign, during which they give away free reflective materials. They may also provide information booklets, posters or a video on winter road safety. The commonly agreed rules for being seen are: Always wear something bright when you go outside – especially at night, on dark days or in poor weather. By day, bright or fluorescent clothes show up best. By night, reflective materials are best and show up in car headlights.

Learning Objectives

Children should:

- know that shiny objects are not light sources.
- know that shiny objects need a light source if they are to shine.
- suggest how to test their ideas about which materials show up best at night.
- make observations and simple comparisons.
- say whether what they found out was what they expected.

Resources

- 'Dark area' as described in Lesson 3
- Torch
- Collection of materials (for example, aluminium foil, white paper, fluorescent paper, a reflective arm band, tinsel)
- Access to a space that can be made fairly dark where the whole class can fit
- Adult helper
- 'Be Safe, Be Seen' poster (and, if possible, other winter road safety materials)
- Reflective materials (for example, arm bands)
- A3 paper
- Colouring pens or pencils

Introduction

Remind the children of the activities carried out previously and ask: *Is it easy to see things in the dark?* As they may now be travelling to and from school in the dark, ask why it is important for other people (especially motorists) to be able to see them. Discuss what they can do to make themselves more visible in the dark. Look at the collection of materials and ask the children to predict which one will be seen the best in the dark. Record their predictions, then ask them to suggest ways of testing these (for example, 'Put them in a dark place and shine a light on them').

Main Activity

Carry out the test as a teacher-led demonstration. *Which material shows up best in the dark? Which shows up least well? Was this what you expected? Which of these things would be best to wear to help motorists see you at night? Would the objects shine if no light is shone on them?* Explain that you will be finding out the answer to this question later.

Show the children the 'Be Safe, Be Seen' poster. Discuss how the poster is designed, concentrating on the image and the slogan. Discuss ideas for other images and slogans that could be used and record these. Ask children to design their own posters that include an image and a slogan.

While the children design their posters, take groups into the 'dark area'. Take in samples of the 'winning' material from your earlier test, and a torch. Observe that the material does not shine at all when it is completely dark and there is no other source of light. *Is it a light source? How do you know?* Finally, shine the torch on the material. *Is it shining now? What does a shiny object need before it can shine?* (A light source)

Plenary

Show and discuss examples of the children's safety posters. Look at any other road safety materials that you have managed to acquire.

What to Look For

Children recognise that a shiny object needs a light source if it is to shine. They explain that a shiny object will not shine in a dark room. They say whether they expected the reflective strips to shine near a light source. When testing different reflective materials the children describe their observations and make comparisons.

What Do We Know About Light and Dark?

Science Background

This lesson offers an opportunity to assess the children's individual understanding of the work covered in this unit.

Learning Objective

Children should:
- demonstrate their understanding of Unit 1D.

Resources

- Large paper for drawing or painting
- Coloured pens and pencils
- Paints and painting equipment
- Pupil sheet D5

Introduction

Tell the children that they are going to draw or paint a picture that shows day on one side and night on the other. Show them how to divide the paper in half. *What might you see at night-time?* Ask them to draw or paint on one half of the paper as many things as they can that they might see at night. Repeat your instructions for the daytime side. Explain that you want them to work on their own so that you can find out what they have learned.

Main Activity

As they work, discuss with children what their pictures or paintings show. Encourage them to show as many things as possible by prompting them about aspects of the picture that they may have overlooked. For example, ask: *Can you add any more light sources to your painting? What colours will you use on your night-time side?*

Plenary

Play the quiz on Pupil sheet D5 by reading out the questions to the children and asking them to put their hands up when you read out the correct answer. You may need to repeat each question several times. This game could be played in mixed-ability teams.

What to Look For

The children produce a drawing or painting which makes a clear distinction between night and day. They can answer quiz questions on the topic correctly.

Light Quiz

D5

1. Which of these things is a light source?

   a) a mirror   b) a gas lighter   c) a reflective arm band

2. Which is the brightest light source?

   a) a torch   b) a candle   c) the Sun

3. Name another light source that hasn't been mentioned yet.

   (Ask each team for a different one.)

4. When do light sources show up best?

   a) when it's the weekend   b) when it's dark   c) when it's light

5. What sense can you use to help you find something in the dark?

   a) touch and hearing   b) taste and smell   c) sight and hearing

6. You can only see things if there is ...

   a) a shadow   b) darkness   c) light

7. Things are easier to see if the light is ...

   a) brighter   b) dimmer   c) smaller

8. A shiny object will only shine if ...

   a) it is flat   b) it is in the dark   c) a light source shines on it

9. To be seen after dark you should wear ...

   a) tinsel   b) reflective patches   c) a white coat

10. At night-time colours are ...

    a) harder to see than during the day   b) easier to see than during the day

    c) just the same as during the day

Unit E

Pushes and Pulls

Scientific Enquiry: • Ask questions and decide how they might find answers to them.
Physical Processes: • Find out about, and describe the movement of, familiar things (for example, cars going faster, slowing down, changing direction). • Recognise that when things speed up, slow down or change direction, there is a cause (for example, a push or a pull).
Approximate Teaching Time: 7 hours

Assessment Grid

Unit 1E

	At level 1, children typically:	**At level 2, children typically:**	**At level 3, children typically:**
Physical Processes	• communicate observations of changes in movement that result from actions (for example, pushing and pulling objects).	• know about a range of physical phenomena and recognise and describe similarities and differences associated with them. • compare the movement of different objects in terms of speed or direction.	• use their knowledge and understanding of physical phenomena to link *cause* and *effect* in simple explanations (for example, the direction of an object changing because of a push or a pull). • begin to make simple generalisations about physical phenomena.

How Do Things Move?

Science Background

This lesson focuses on observing and describing the different types of movement performed by people and machines. Elements of movement that should be described are the type (for example, rolling, turning, jumping; the direction (up, down, on the spot, left, right, backwards, forwards); the speed (fast, slow); and the acceleration (slowing down, constant speed, speeding up).

Learning Objectives

Children should:

- know that there are many sorts of movement which can be described in many ways.
- observe and describe different ways of moving.

Resources

- A space for movement
- A list of words to describe movement (e.g. *type*: slide, bounce, jump, swing, turn, rock, roll, wave, twist, jog, run, walk, crawl, hang, stand, sit; *direction*: raise, lower, left, right, forwards, backwards, diagonally, on the spot; *speed and acceleration*: fast, slow, get faster, stay the same speed, get slower)
- A varied collection of moving toys
- Battery-operated clock with second hand
- Pupil sheet E1

Introduction

Play the singing game 'One finger, one thumb keep moving'. Add various different body parts to the song and ask the children to suggest other body parts that move, and find a way of adding these to it. For a fun challenge, see who can move the end of their nose or wiggle their ears without touching them.

Main Activity

In a space big enough for the whole class to move around freely, choose a movement word and ask children to move in that way (see the list in Resources, above). Next, give the children movement instructions that incorporate two or more elements (for example: *Do a twisting movement that slows down*; *Do a fast bounce on the spot*; *Slide slowly sideways*; *Move your arms in a swaying motion*) .

Show the children the collection of moving toys and ask individuals to help you to demonstrate how they move. Ask the class to identify the parts of each toy that move, and to suggest words that describe how the toys move (for example, 'bouncing', 'spinning', 'rolling', 'rocking'). Compare the speed and direction of movement of different toys, and ask whether any of the movements are speeding up or slowing down.

Discuss Pupil sheet E1 with the children. Ask them to match the descriptive phrases to the pictures.

Differentiation: More able children could be given a copy of the sheet without the word list. Less able readers may need support.
Extension: Children could draw and label more of their own 'movement cartoons'.

Plenary

Look at an everyday machine that is moving (for example, a wall clock with a second hand). *Which parts of the object are moving?* (The hands) Ask them to describe the type and direction of the movement (turning, clockwise) and the speed of the movement (one fast second hand; one slower minute hand and one even slower hour hand).
Is the movement of the second hand speeding up, slowing down or staying at the same speed? Where does the energy come from for the movement? (The battery) *Where does the energy come from for your movement?* (Muscles, which in turn get their power from food)

What to Look For
Children can describe the movement of objects using appropriate words and phrases. They can describe a series of movements they make and can make a series of movements matching a description given by another person.

RS

Word Cards for Unit 1E

moving	move
push	pull
start	stop
faster	slower
human	engine
mains electricity	wind
water	battery
windmill	wind turbine

How Do We Move?

E1

Name: ____________________ Date: ____________________

- Match the words with the pictures.
  The first one has been done for you.
  The last two boxes are for your own pictures.

hopping			

jumping	swinging	bouncing
running	crawling	climbing
rolling	spinning	sliding

Starting and Stopping

Science Background

A force is defined as a push or a pull. For movement to be initiated, a force must act upon an object. The larger the force, the more the object will accelerate and the further it will move. Through discussion, help the children to reach generalisations about how the toys move (for example, 'The harder you push the faster it goes', 'The gentler you push the slower it goes').

Learning Objectives

Children should:

- know that pushing or pulling things can make objects start or stop moving.
- make suggestions about how objects can be made to move.
- find out whether their predictions were right.
- recognise hazards in moving objects.

Resources

- Sticky notes
- A variety of wheeled toys
- String
- Masking tape
- Enough ramps for one per group
- A variety of surfaces to roll the toys over (for example, carpet tiles, vinyl floor tiles, blankets, sandpaper)

Introduction

Write the words 'push' and 'pull' on the board. Read them together and, as you do so, perform actions for each one. Remind the children that pushing means moving things away, and pulling means moving things towards you. Allow pairs to experiment with moving objects in the classroom for a few minutes. Prompt them to label each object they test with sticky notes on which they have written 'push', 'pull' or 'push and pull'.

Differentiation: Less able writers could be given a set of pre-written notes.

Main Activity

Divide the class into small groups and give each group a wheeled toy. Show them the other resources available to them.

Challenge 1: *In how many different ways can you start the toy moving?* (For example, push, pull, put at the top of a ramp and let go, attach a string and pull it.) Before they start this challenge, ask the children to predict how many different ways they might find. When they have finished the test ask: *Could you start the toy moving in the ways you suggested? Did you find any other ways of starting the toy moving that you didn't think of before?*

Challenge 2: *Can you make the toy move more slowly?* (For example, roll it on a rougher or squashier surface, push it more gently, pull the string more slowly.) *Can you make it travel further?* (For example, push it harder, put it on a ramp, roll it on a smoother or harder surface.) *Can you make it change direction while it is moving?* (For example, roll it up a ramp so that it rolls back down again.) Discuss with the children what they have found out.

Challenge 3: *In how many different ways can you stop the toy moving?* (For example, run it into an obstacle, push down on it, pull on a string attached at the back.)

Plenary

Ask the children to demonstrate the various ways they have found of stopping the wheeled toys. *What sorts of moving objects would it be unsafe to try to stop?* (For example, swings, roundabouts, bicycles other people are riding, skateboards, supermarket trolleys, cars, etc.) *What could happen if you tried to stop these objects?*

What to Look For

Children identify objects which they moved by pushing and those which they moved by pulling. They say whether their predictions about getting an object moving were correct. They describe how an object might be stopped. They explain why it can be dangerous to try to stop some moving objects.

What Makes It Move?

Science Background

Anything which provides the energy needed for movement is called a 'power source'. While children do not need to know this term at this stage, they do need to be able to identify the power sources that make familiar objects move. The list on Pupil sheet E3 is not meant to be comprehensive, but reflects some of the most common power sources.

Learning Objectives

Children should:

- know that it is not only ourselves that make things move by pushing .
- ask questions about what is causing movement.

Resources

- A toy windmill
- An electric fan
- A toy water wheel
- A jug of water
- A bowl
- A battery-powered moving toy
- An electrical appliance where movement can be seen (for example, tape player)
- A soft ball
- Word cards with pictures: 'human', 'engine', 'battery', 'mains electricity', 'the wind', 'water'
- Scissors and glue sticks
- Equipment for blowing bubbles
- Resource Sheet 'What Makes It Move?'
- Pupil sheet E3

Introduction

Recap previous work by asking the children to tell you the different ways in which they can make things move. Explain that it's not just people that can make things move. Demonstrate the objects below moving, asking volunteers to help you. For each object, ask: *What's making it move?* Demonstrate the toy waterwheel (water), the toy windmill using the electric fan (wind), the battery-powered moving toy (an electric battery), the tape player (mains electricity) and the soft ball (a human). *Who came to school in a car this morning? What makes the car move?* (Engine) When each power source has been identified, display the relevant word card on the board. At the end of the activity, reread the word cards, asking the children to name something that can be made to move in that way.

Main Activity

Display large copies or transparencies of Resource Sheet 'What Makes It Move?' and Pupil sheet E3. Explain how to complete the Pupil sheet by cutting out the pictures on the Resource Sheet and sticking them in the right boxes. Through discussion, decide where a few of the pictures should go. Give each child a copy of each sheet and ask children to work individually to complete it.

Differentiation: Less able children could work in pairs. Ask children who finish to add a few of their own drawings in each box.
Extension: Ask the children to record their ideas about anything else that can make other things move.

Plenary

Take the children outside and blow bubbles. Ask them to describe what happens to the bubbles after they blow them (they move). *What is making the bubbles move?* (The wind), *Can you see the wind?* (No), *How can you tell that the wind is blowing?* (Because it makes the bubbles and other things move), *What is the wind?* (It's the air moving).

What to Look For
Children understand that it is not just humans that can make things move. They can identify the cause of motion in moving objects.

RS

What Makes It Move?

What Makes It Move?

E3

Name: ______________________ Date: ______________

a human	an engine	a battery
mains electricity	**the wind**	**water**

Windmills

Science Background

Useful information on wind power is currently available on the British Wind Energy Association website at www.bwea.com. There is a teachers' section with free downloadable resources, including an information booklet and pupil activities.

Learning Objective

Children should:

- observe and describe different ways of moving.
- identify similarities and differences between the movement of different objects.
- know that it is not only ourselves that make things move by pushing.

Resources

- A copy of the poem 'Who Has Seen the Wind?' by Christina Rosetti
- Animations or video footage of windmills and wind turbines
- Pre-made windmill from Resource Sheet 'Windmills'
- Half-made windmill which has been cut out and decorated on both sides
- Coloured-paper copies of Resource Sheet 'Windmills'
- Collage materials
- Coloured pencils and crayons
- Scissors
- Drawing pins
- Erasers
- Lengths of dowelling or garden sticks
- A hammer
- Ribbons or crêpe paper
- Sticky tape, glue

Introduction

Read together the poem 'Who Has Seen the Wind?' by Christina Rosetti. Ask the children to name other things that can be moved by the wind.

Main Activity

Show the children the animations or video footage of windmills and wind turbines. *What are these machines called? What is the same about how they move?* (They turn round and round.) *What is different about how they move? What makes them move?* (The wind) *What are they used for?* (The windmill for grinding wheat to make flour, and the wind turbine to make electricity.) Ask whether anyone has ever seen a windmill or a wind turbine close up.

Show the windmill that you have made. Next, show the half-made windmill and explain how to make it. Ask the children to cut the windmill out, including cutting along all the lines, then decorate both sides of the paper using different colours or patterns on each side. Once a few children have done this, demonstrate how to attach the drawing pin through the centre of the windmill and press it into an eraser to hold it together. The final stage, hammering the drawing pin to a piece of dowelling, should be done by an adult. The dowelling could be decorated with coloured ribbons or thin strips of crêpe paper.

Plenary

Test the windmills. *How many different ways can you make your windmill move?* (For example, push it, pull it, blow on it.) *How can you make it spin faster?* (Blow, push or pull harder.) *or slower?* (Blow, push or pull more gently.) *How can you stop your windmill? Does everyone's windmill move in the same direction?* (No, because some face one way and will only be blown in one direction and others face the other way and will only be blown in the opposite direction.) Finally, take the windmills outside and test them in the wind.

What to Look For

Children describe the movement of windmills and wind turbines. They identify similarities and differences between their movements. They know that the wind causes them to move.

⚠ Care is needed when attaching the drawing pins to the dowelling. It usually requires a significant force, and you may even need to use a hammer. It should only be undertaken by an adult.

Windmills

RS

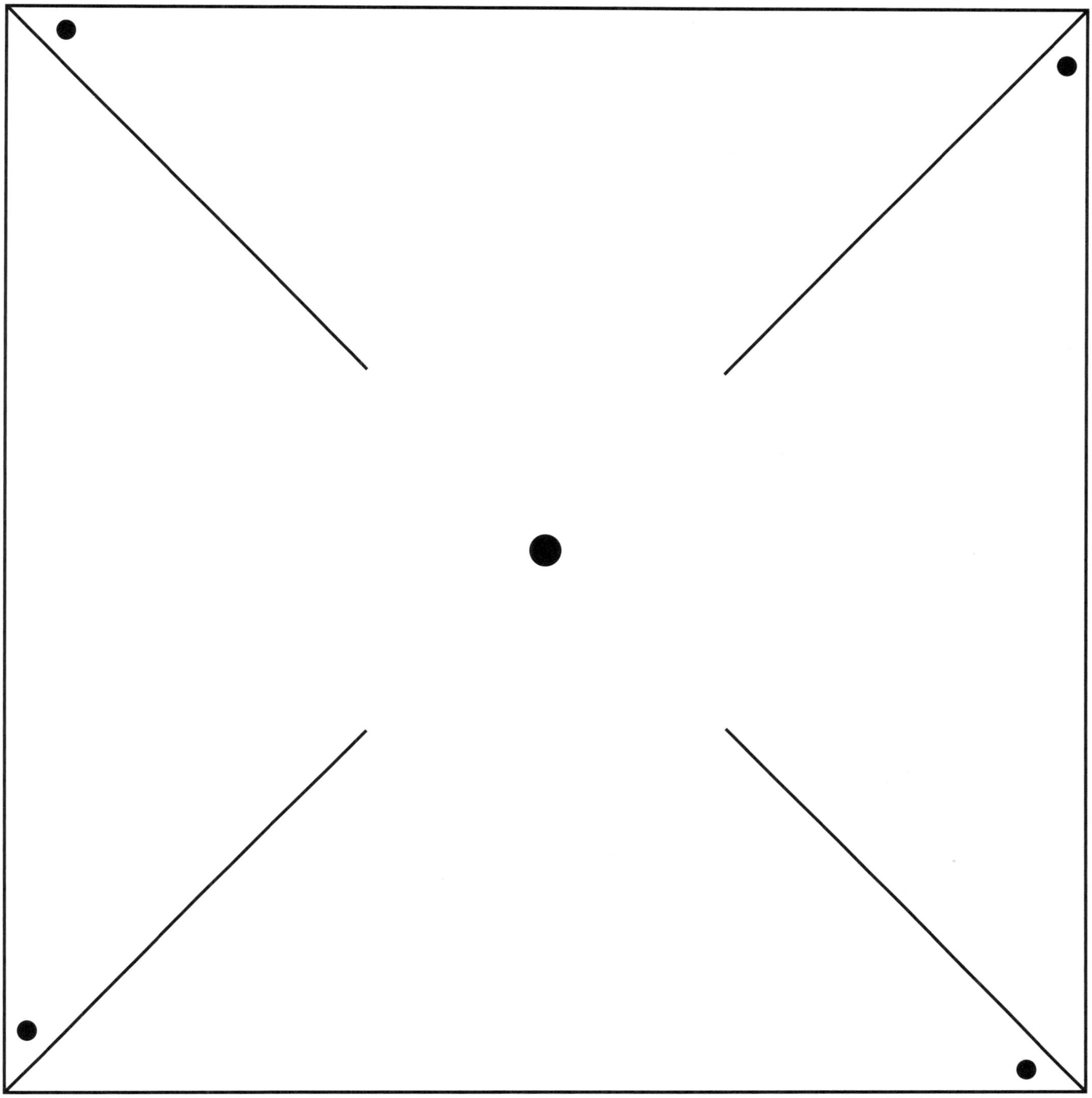

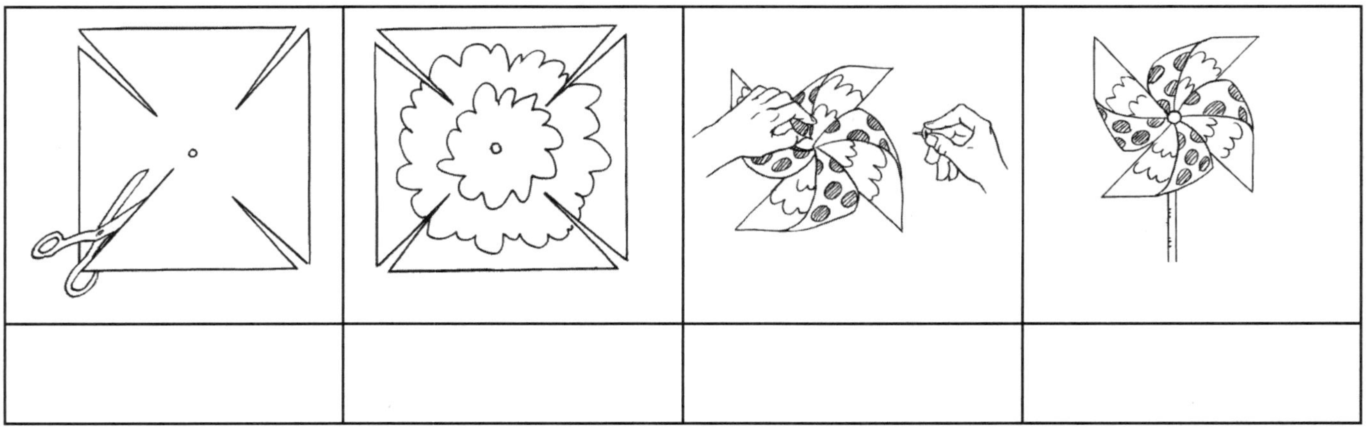

Unit F

Sound and Hearing

Scientific Enquiry: ● Ask questions and decide how they might find answers to them. ● Follow simple instructions to control the risks to themselves and to others. ● Explore, using the senses of sight, hearing, smell, touch and taste as appropriate, and make and record observations and measurements. ● Communicate what happened in a variety of ways. ● Make simple comparisons and identify simple patterns or associations. ● Compare what happened with what they expected would happen, and try to explain it, drawing on their knowledge and understanding. ● Review their work and explain what they did to others.
Life and Living Processes: ● Know about the senses that enable humans and other animals to be aware of the world around them.
Physical Processes: ● Know that there are many kinds of sound and sources of sound. ● Know that sounds travel away from sources, getting fainter as they do so, and that they are heard when they enter the ear.
Approximate Teaching Time: 7 hours

Assessment Grid

Unit 1F

	At level 1, children typically:	At level 2, children typically:	At level 3, children typically:
Physical Processes	• communicate observations of changes in sound that result from actions. • recognise that sound comes from a variety of sources and name some of these.	• compare the loudness or pitch of sounds.	• use their knowledge and understanding of physical phenomena to link *cause* and *effect* in simple explanations. • begin to make simple generalisations about physical phenomena (for example, explaining that sounds they hear become fainter the further they are from the source).

Identifying Sounds

Science Background

Anything that makes a sound is called a 'sound source'. Sighted people rarely use their sense of hearing in isolation, relying instead on a combination of auditory and visual clues to identify sounds. Identifying unseen sound sources can be difficult, even for adults. Listening effectively is a skill which takes lots of practice and which few children have sufficient opportunities to develop fully. Learning to sit quietly and concentrate all their attention on the sounds they hear, without being distracted by visual stimuli, can be very challenging.

Learning Objectives

Children should:

- know that there are many different sources of sounds.
- explore sounds using their sense of hearing.
- identify sounds by listening carefully.

Resources

- Large sheet of paper (flipchart size)
- Flipchart marker
- Sound effects CD or tape
- CD or tape player
- Toy crown (optional)

Introduction

Take the class on a 'listening walk' around the school and grounds. Take a large sheet of paper and a flipchart marker with you. Stop in different place. Ask the children to listen carefully for about a minute and to make a mental note of all the sounds they hear. (You might like to suggest they close their eyes.) When time is up, ask the children to tell you everything they heard. On the sheet of large paper, note each location and the sounds the children identify there.

Main Activity

Back in the classroom, review the results of the listening walk. Ask questions about the data collected, for example: *How many different sounds did we hear altogether? Which sounds did we hear in more than one place? In which place did we hear the most sounds? In which place did we hear the fewest sounds? Was this what you expected?*

Play a sound quiz game. Divide the class into two or more teams. Listen to selected tracks from the sound effects CD or tape. Listening to one sound at a time, ask one person from each team to identify the sound. Award a point for each correct answer.

Plenary

Play 'Greetings, Your Majesty'. Choose one child to be the King or Queen and to stand at the front of the class with their eyes closed and their back to the other children. (They could wear a toy crown, if you have one.) Choose a volunteer to say, 'Greetings, Your Majesty'. Then the King or Queen turns around and tries to guess who spoke. If they guess correctly they remain King or Queen and they get another go. If they are wrong, then the child who spoke becomes the King or Queen. (Once the children get the hang of the game they could try to disguise their voices.)

What to Look For

Children identify a range of familiar sounds. They listen carefully to identify different speakers.

RS

Word Cards for Unit 1F

listen	sounds
high	low
long	short
fast	slow
quiet	loud
hit	shake
blow	scrape
hear	further

Making and Describing Sounds

Science Background

Sounds can be described in terms of pitch, speed, duration, volume and timbre (the character and quality of a sound). For example, the timbre of a sound might be described as woody, metallic, breathy, rounded, flat, bright, dull, etc. Timbre is the hardest to explain to children, but is usually the most interesting for them to describe because it encourages a creative and multi-sensory approach to the use of vocabulary. Even young children can sometimes come up with descriptions that are beautifully poetic.

Learning Objectives

Children should:

- know that there are many different ways of making sounds.
- present and interpret results.
- know that there are many ways of describing sounds.

Resources

- For each table: a selection of musical instruments and other everyday objects that make sounds when they are shaken, hit, scraped or blown (for example, tambourine, sleigh bells, whistle, recorder, maracas, claves, guiro, corrugated cardboard, baby's rattle, bicycle bell)
- A different collection of about six instruments and other sound-making objects for the Introduction
- Reference materials about musical instruments
- Pupil sheet F2 (one copy enlarged to A3)
- Resource Sheet 'Sounds Word Bank'

Introduction

Show the children the collection of instruments and objects and, taking one item at a time, ask them to identify it and then to suggest how they might make a sound with it. Ask a child to come to the front and test out these ideas. Using a large copy of Pupil sheet F2, ask another child to draw the instrument or object in the correct section of the chart. Make it clear that some instruments or objects should be drawn in more than one section (for example, a tambourine can be shaken or hit).

Main Activity

Ask the children to sort the instruments on their table in the same way.

Differentiation: Provide more able groups with a larger number of instruments. They could also be given items that do not fit neatly into any of the first four categories (for example, something which is played by plucking, like a toy guitar).
Extension: Using appropriate reference materials, extend the children by asking them to find out how other musical instruments make sounds, and add them to their chart.

Gather the class together with their completed Pupil sheets. Encourage them to interpret the data they have collected by asking questions such as: *How many instruments or objects are in each group? Which group has the most instruments or objects in it? Which group has the least?* Once more, bring the children's attention to the instruments and objects used in the Introduction. This time, ask them to listen to the sound each instrument or object makes, and to suggest ways of describing it (for example, 'high' or 'low', 'long' or 'short', 'fast' or 'slow', 'quiet' or 'loud', 'rattling', 'ringing', etc.) Write the children's descriptive words around the relevant picture on the large version of the chart. Allow them time to listen to the sounds made by the instruments and objects on their tables and to add descriptive words to their copies of the Resource Sheet.

Differentiation: Provide less able writers with a word bank. Use Resource Sheet 'Sounds Word Bank'.

Plenary

Ask the children to give an example of a sound that they like. Encourage them to describe the sound and explain why they like it. Repeat the activity, this time asking children to name and describe sounds that they dislike.

What to Look For

Children identify different ways in which simple musical instruments and other objects make sounds. They group instruments and objects and compare how many there are in each group. They describe sounds using appropriate vocabulary. They recognise that some sounds give us pleasure and others do not.

F2

Making and Describing Sounds

Name: ______________________ Date: ______________________

You **hit** these.
You **shake** these.
You **blow** these.
You **scrape** these.
You **do something else** with these.

Sounds Word Bank

RS

a	b banging bouncing breathy bright	c clapping clicking continnuous crashing crunching	d deep drumming dull
e echoing	f fast flat fluttering	g	h high howling
i	j jumping	k knocking	l lasting long louds low
m metallic musical	n noisy	o	p piercing
q quick quiet quivering	r rattling ringing rolling rounded rumbling	s screeching sharp short singing sliding soft squealing stuttering	t tapping ticking tinkling tinny thudding thumping twanging
u	v	w whistling windy wooden	x, y, z

Hearing Sounds

Science Background

Sound is created when an object vibrates. This causes the air around it to vibrate. These vibrations in the air, known as sound waves, are collected by the outer ear, travel down the ear canal and strike the eardrum. From here they pass to the small bones of the middle ear, which transmit them to the auditory nerve in the inner ear. The auditory nerve connects directly to the brain. At this age, children need to know simply that sound travels through the air and we hear it when it reaches our ears.

Learning Objectives

Children should:

- know that we hear with our ears.
- turn ideas about hearing into ideas that can be tested.
- make and record observations and present them in drawings and writing.
- understand that we use our sense of hearing for a range of purposes, including recognising hazards and risks.

Resources

- Paper or science books
- Blindfolds (one per group)
- Musical instruments (one per group)
- Road safety video
- Resource Sheet 'Hearing Sounds' (enlarged to A3 or as an OHT)

Introduction

Allow the children five minutes to draw a picture on paper or in their science books showing how they think we hear sounds. Then, as a class, ask some children to explain their drawings and together discuss their ideas.

Display the enlarged copy of Resource Sheet 'Hearing Sounds', which shows how we hear sounds. Explain that sound travels through the air from a sound source and we hear it when it reaches our ears.

Main Activity

Blindfold one child and ask another child to take an instrument and play it. The blindfolded child tries to guess where the sound is coming from and points in the right direction. Ask the children: *How could we make the game harder?* Discuss the children's ideas. For example, they might suggest covering both ears, covering one ear, playing the instrument more quietly or moving the instrument further away. Record these ideas on the board in notes or pictures. Ask the children to predict what they think will happen. Organise small groups to try the ideas out and record what happens using drawings and writing.

Differentiation: Less able groups may need adult support to carry out the tests and record their results.

When the children have finished working, review all the ideas that they have tested and ask: *What happened when you tried this idea? What did you find out from this?*

Plenary

Show the children a short road safety video and ask why hearing is important when crossing the road. Ask them to suggest other situations in which being able to hear sounds and work out where they are coming from might help us to keep safe.

What to Look For

Children know that they hear sounds through their ears. They recognise that our ears also give information about where sounds are coming from. They suggest how to find out about hearing.

RS

Hearing Sounds

Sound travels through the air.

We hear it when it reaches our ears.

Sounds Near and Far

Science Background

Children need to know that a sound is always loudest at the source and gets quieter the further it travels from the source, until eventually it cannot be heard. This lesson concentrates on teaching skills and techniques in experimental and investigative work which the children will be applying in the next lesson.

Learning Objective

Children should:

- know that some sounds can be heard from a long distance.
- know that sounds seem louder the nearer you are to the source.
- know that sounds get fainter as they travel away from a source.
- measure distances using standard measures.

Resources

- Sound source with a consistent volume (for example, electric buzzer)
- A day that is dry and not too windy
- Metre sticks (at least two)
- Flipchart or board
- Clipboard, pencil and paper
- Interlocking cubes
- Resource Sheet 'Sounds' (enlarged to A3 or as an OHT)

Introduction

Show the children the copy of Resource Sheet 'Sounds'. *Which sounds can be heard from far away? Why is that?* (Because they are loud.) Label the sound sources on the sheet 'quiet' and 'loud', as appropriate. Ask the children to describe what it is like to be near one of the very loud sounds. Discuss safety issues relating to loud sound sources (for example, why people who work with loud equipment need to wear ear protectors).

Main Activity

Play a fairly quiet sound source that produces a sound of a consistent volume (for example, an electric buzzer). Ask the children: *Is this sound quiet or loud? Do you think you could hear it from a long way away? How far away do you think you would be able to hear the buzzer?* Write this last question on a flipchart or board. Show the class the metre stick and ask: *How far is this?* Ask them to estimate how many sticks (metres) away they think they will hear the buzzer. It doesn't matter if their predictions are wildly inaccurate! Record their ideas so that you can refer to them in the Plenary.

Ask the children how they might find out the answer to the question on the board, and help them to plan the test. *Will you start close to the sound source and move further away, or start far away and move closer? Will the person with the sound source move or will everyone else? What will you measure?* (For example, the number of children who can hear the buzzer at different distances.) *Which distances will you collect data for? How will you record the data? Who will do what?* Once the test is planned, take the children outside and help them to carry it out.

Plenary

Back in the classroom, create a chart of results (perhaps using towers of interlocking cubes, one cube representing one child, colour-coded for different distances). Ask questions about the data, for example: *When was it easiest to hear the buzzer?* (When it was closest.) *Why?* (Because it sounded louder.) *Was the sound that the buzzer made actually louder?* (No, it just sounded louder because it was closer.) *When was it hardest to hear the buzzer?* (When it was furthest away.) *Why?* (Because it sounded quieter.) *Was the sound that the buzzer made actually quieter?* (No, it just sounded quieter because it was further away.) *Were your predictions right?*

What to Look For

Children identify some very loud sounds and recognise that they can be harmful. They recognise these sounds are louder when they are nearer to the source.

RS

Sounds

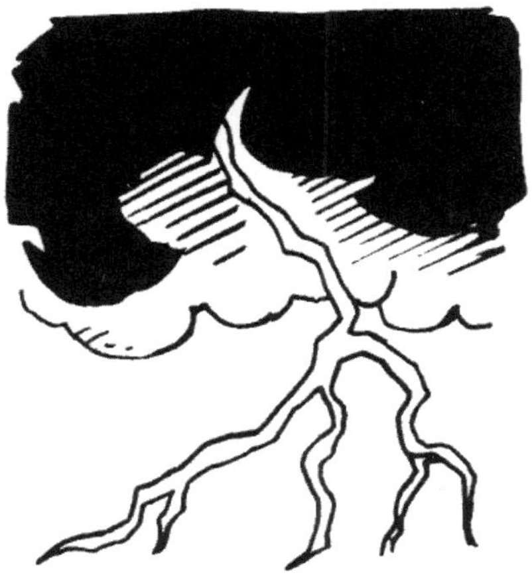

Investigating Sounds

Science Background

Sounds seem quieter from a distance because as sound waves move outwards from the source, their energy spreads out through an ever greater volume of air and therefore an ever smaller proportion of that energy reaches your ears. Eventually the amount of sound energy reaching your ears is too small to be detected, and you can no longer hear the sound. Louder sounds travel further because their sound waves start off with more energy.

Learning Objective

Children should:

- make and record measurements.
- present results using diagrams or charts.
- make comparisons between results.
- draw conclusions from results.

Resources

- Variety of musical instruments and other sound sources, arranged in pairs (one loud and one quiet)
- Labels reading 'loud' and 'quiet' (for example, on sticky notes)
- Standard or non-standard measuring equipment
- A large, blank bar chart to show one aspect of the data collected by the class (for example, a graph with two bars, one labelled 'quiet' and one 'loud', to show which sound each child could hear from further away)
- Pupil sheet F5

Introduction

Show the children two sound sources and ask them to tell you which one they think will be louder and which one quieter. Ask two volunteers to play the sound sources one after the other. Ask another child to label one object 'loud' and one 'quiet'. *Which sound do you think will travel further, the loud sound or the quiet sound?*

Main Activity

Explain to the children that they will be working in groups to find out whether loud sounds or quiet sounds travel further. Ask them for their ideas about how to carry out the test. If they get stuck, suggest that one person plays the quiet sound source and another stands close by. The listener should then gradually move away from the sound source. As soon as they can't hear it any more they should stop moving. The third person then measures the distance between the sound source and the listener (either in standard or non-standard units), and records it on the Pupil sheet. Ask them to swap jobs until everyone has had a turn at being the listener, and then repeat the whole test using the loud sound source. Demonstrate how to fill in the Pupil sheet.

Organise groups of three, giving each group a pair of sound sources (one quiet and one loud) and a copy of the Pupil sheet. Ask them to listen to the sounds the sound sources make and label them with the sticky notes before they start work on their test.

As this activity is potentially very noisy, it may be a good idea to spread it out over the course of a few sessions so that only one or two groups are tackling it at any one time.

Plenary

Ask the children questions that require them to read and interpret their results, for example: *Was everyone in the group the same distance from the sound when they stopped hearing it? Why do you think this is?*

Show the children the blank bar chart that you have prepared. Ask them to help you fill in their personal data. Ask them questions about the data represented in the bar chart, for example: *Which sound travelled further? How do you know? Is this what you thought would happen?*

What to Look For

Children make and record measurements using standard or non-standard measures. They contribute to a chart presenting results. They compare measurements with each other. They compare how far they were from the two sources when they stopped hearing them. They state that they could hear the louder sound further away than the quieter sound.

Which Sound Travels Further?

F5

Name: ______________________ Date: ______________________

	This is our quiet sound:	This is our loud sound:
Names	couldn't hear the quiet sound after	couldn't hear the loud sound after

Area of Science	Level				Comments
Unit A: Ourselves					
Scientific Enquiry	W	1	2	3	
Humans and Other Animals	W	1	2	3	
Unit B: Growing Plants					
Scientific Enquiry	W	1	2	3	
Green Plants	W	1	2	3	
Unit C: Sorting and Using Materials					
Scientific Enquiry	W	1	2	3	
Grouping Materials	W	1	2	3	
Unit D: Light and Dark					
Scientific Enquiry	W	1	2	3	
Light and Sound	W	1	2	3	
Unit E: Pushes and Pulls					
Scientific Enquiry	W	1	2	3	
Forces and Motion	W	1	2	3	
Unit F: Sound and Hearing					
Scientific Enquiry	W	1	2	3	
Light and Sound	W	1	2	3	